FEASTS OF FAITH

FINDING JESUS IN THE JEWISH FEASTS

BY DALLAS AND CARL PAETZOLD

Feasts of Faith
— Finding Jesus in the Jewish Feasts

Published by PCG Legacy
A division of Pilot Communications Group, Inc.

ISBN: 978-1-936417-19-3

Unless otherwise noted, all Scripture is quoted from *The New American Standard Bible*. (1977). LaHabra California: The Lockman Foundation.

Authors' photo by: Laurie Paetzold
Cover design by: Tony Clayton

Printed in the United States of America

Contact the authors:

Carl & Dallas Paetzold:
www.FeastsofFaith.com

Dedication

From Carl and Dallas:

To our kids Paris, Connor, Carson, and Cooper for dragging along all sorts of Jewish paraphernalia, reading the four questions and searching for afikomen during all seasons of the year in all sorts of churches, and for encouraging us to "just write down what you know." You guys are amazing!

From Dallas:

To my sisters, Beverly and Lisa,
Who share my brain
And to the memory of our parents and grandparents
Who lived out their faith and shared it with us over many family feasts

ACKNOWLEDGMENTS

This book has been 10 years in the making and so many people have had such a grand impact on our lives and on this book coming to fruition. Our great thanks and appreciation to our dear friends in Bible studies, prayer groups, and small groups who have continuously encouraged us by asking about our progress and by praying specifically for each step throughout this project.

Our special thanks to:

Zvi Rivai, our amazing Messianic Jewish Israeli tour guide, who graciously edited the original manuscript for historical and Jewish accuracy, and overwhelmed us with his knowledge and love for Israel. Any mistakes in these areas are solely ours.

Beverly Larson, for allowing us a quiet place to write in her home, for reading and re-reading, for texting encouragement and for sharing the dream by contributing some of her own beautiful writing to this project. Words fail us in attempting to convey the incredible inspiration you've been to us.

All of our Encouragement Café friends who prayed, encouraged, believed, and exhorted us to finally get this published. Thanks for rooting for us.

Arlene, Melody and Susan who have spent countless hours in the last 10 years hearing about and praying over this book. You are more like sisters than friends. Thank you.

Tony Clayton, one of the most talented people we know, for believing in the content, designing the cover, giving us the title, and cheering us on at the very end.

Mario & Lynelle Zandstra with Pine Cove Christian Camps, for assuring us that "normal people" could write a book and for recommending Brian Mast at Pilot Communications Group. Brian, anything that seemed easy was because of you! Thank you.

Amy Seeger, for editing the text and for helping us transform a study guide into a book. You are truly gifted.

The sweet friends who have blessed our lives and have allowed us to share their stories: Susan, Amy, Heather, Kyle & Bernita, and Callie & D'Lynn.

Brandon Coleman, Carl's nephew, for finding our lost chapters in a matter of minutes. You are a computer genius, Brandon, thank you!

And the David Family, whom we've never met, but through their generosity allowed us time at "the Shack" to write. You've blessed us!

Finally, to our Lord and Savior, Jesus Christ, Who makes all things possible.

Contents

Introduction

We watched the spring thunderstorm rolling into the Texas Panhandle, truly a majestic and powerful beauty to behold. Plenty of sky and few trees make for a massive, unhindered canvas. Expansive brushstrokes of monstrous dark blue and green clouds swept away the lighter blue sky as the storm built and made its way across the dusty landscape. Here and there, bright yellow, narrow rays of sunshine flashed forcefully through the imposing cloud ceiling, allowing us a glimpse into God's magnificent sanctuary. Unfortunately, all was not calm under this glorious canopy.

"Grab the hanging plants off of the porch and get them inside!" Dallas barked to one child, "Lay the rocking chairs over on their sides," she ordered the next child in line. Like little soldiers, each child stepped up to receive the subsequent command. As quickly as the instructions were handed out, they were obeyed; four children dashing about, contributing their part to outracing the storm.

In our part of the country, these types of storms usually have a leading edge of extremely forceful wind. Anything that is not secured may come flying through the window or end up in the next state. Growing up with the endless wind, we didn't know much different. We learned early on to open car doors one at a time, or at least doors only on the same side of the car. Otherwise, the wind would whip right through that car-made tunnel and take every scrap of trash and the baby in the car seat right out the other side!

We never had porch furniture that wasn't wrought iron, and it certainly didn't have any cushions on it. Those outdoor tablecloths with the little weights on each corner were only good for knocking out a window when the wind whipped the whole thing off the table, swirling it through the air, narrowly missing Grandma and sending it crashing right back through the kitchen window inside where it belonged. One of the idiosyncrasies of the Panhandle is that the trees grow with a slight, permanent bend from the prevailing winds. And living here, you learn quickly to be discerning about whether or not to wear Chapstick or lip gloss. Is it really worth licking mud off your lips all day?

Our local high school's mascot is a "sandie," as in a sandstorm, and their cheer is, "Blow, sand, blow!" Not a hard thing to accomplish here. When we moved to North Carolina, it was several months before we quit subconsciously shielding our heads as we walked past the neighbors' wicker chairs sitting in their yard. We just knew those things were going to be lifted up with the wind and slam us from behind … but they never moved! The wind rarely blows in North Carolina. We would chuckle at the newscasters as they announced a 20 mph wind advisory and warned viewers to bring in their small pets.

When we moved back to the Texas Panhandle three years later, we were met with the daily 20 mph wind and thanked God that it was a calm day for West Texas. We did, however, notice a strange habit developing in our four-year-old son, Connor, after about the third day we were back in Texas. "Why do you keep putting your arms over your head when we go outside, buddy?" Dallas asked him.

"I'm afraid the wind is gonna blow away my hair," he replied.

It's hard to argue with his good reasoning: After all, he wasn't much bigger than a small pet. We assured him that God had attached the hair to his head with much more power than the wind could blow. We also reminded him that God is so powerful, that He simply walks upon the wings of the wind (Psalm 104:3-4). From that moment on, our little guy decided God must walk around our place quite often!

The storm Dallas and the kids had been watching sweep quickly across the plains that spring day was most likely bringing excessive wind and some hail too. Since we had only one garage and two cars, Carl planned to leave his vehicle in a covered parking area just a couple of miles from our house. Dallas and the kids went to pick him up, and we raced the storm back home. Just as we turned our minivan into our garage, the wind from the leading edge of the storm arrived, and our green plastic, turtle-shaped sandbox went flying straight over the top of the van. It had been weighted down with several bricks awaiting a trip to the store to buy more sand. We never saw the sandbox or the bricks again. We later learned the winds were clocked at 70 mph that day. Funny thing, we never heard a small pet advisory, but that was a windy day even for the Panhandle.

The prevailing winds, the parched ground, the big sky, and the cool starry nights, they are a part of us both. Each of us grew up in this part of the country, our ancestors coaxing crops from the fields. We could tell you loads of wind stories, personal scrapes with tornados, and accounts of the 1930s Dust Bowl passed on to us from our parents and grandparents.

We used to despise the wind until we learned the Hebrew name for the Holy Spirit: Ruach Ha-Kodesh. Now we've learned to embrace the wind, respecting its power, observing its effects, even though we can't see the wind itself. We respect the way the wind changes the events we have planned for the day, whipping us with a strong gust or cooling us by a slight breeze. Yes, the wind reminds us now of the Ruach Ha-Kodesh, in Hebrew sometimes translated: "Holy Wind," or "Holy Breath." Since the Lord spoke to Job out of a whirlwind, asking him if he understood the expanse of the earth, or if he had seen the store-houses of hail, or knew the way of the east wind scattered on the earth, we're of the opinion that God lives somewhere in Texas!

However, He sent His Son to live in Judea as a Jewish boy who would become a great storyteller, teaching people through experiences familiar to them. He led them to understand God and His ways through the heritage passed down to them from Abraham, Isaac, Jacob, and Moses. He taught them by fulfilling in Himself ancient prophecy found in the Hebrews' written word, exhorting them to love and good deeds, educating them from His own familiarity with the traditions of the day, and finally proving Himself as the long-awaited Messiah by becoming the Lamb of God that all the assembly sacrificed at the Feast of Passover. Luke 2:41-52 tells us that Jesus attended this feast with His parents every year in Jerusalem. What details of scripture might we uncover if we ventured back to the time of Jesus? What depth of intimacy, what secret of reverence might we understand if we sat with His family at a Passover meal eating matzah ball soup, or if we tagged along on the pilgrimage to Jerusalem for the Feast of Tabernacles?

Just like each of our families have their own specific peculiarities when it comes to holiday meals, tradition and culture differ among Jewish people depending on the country they live in and the influence of local culture. Traditions also vary based on the time period, changing from generation to generation. The size of their individual families may even contribute to additions and deletions of certain traditions. And, boy, can we identify with that! Dallas and Carl's families vary greatly. Dallas comes from a small family where holiday meals were usually served with the best china and the three of us girls sat at the dining room table with our parents and all of the grandparents discussing quietly the politics of the day or the most recent church sermon. Carl once joked that Dallas' family could have a family reunion in the back of a station wagon!

By comparison, Carl has a large, noisy, laughing family who usually serve a holiday meal buffet style. It's a great rite of passage for a grandchild to "graduate" from the "kids' table" to the "adult table," which typically requires being married and having a child of your own to take your former place at the "kids' table" so you can move up. Cousins race about playing; conversation is demonstrative, funny, and engaging.

Regardless of the atmosphere, both families observe their holidays with purpose. In giving thanks, we eat turkey and dressing on Thanksgiving Day. In celebration of the gift of a Savior, we exchange presents at Christmas. And in celebration of freedom, we shoot off fireworks on the Fourth of July (this last one's always more fun with Carl's family, and usually involves wives running for cover at some point!)

Our goal for this study is to introduce you to Jewish traditions and cultures both past and present. They may occasionally differ from one time period or culture to another. For example, we will sometimes compare Ashkenazic Jews to Sephardic Jews. In 70 A.D., the Jewish temple in Jerusalem was destroyed by Rome. The Jews were then dispersed throughout the world. The Ashkenazic Jews are those from primarily European countries. The Sephardic Jews are those primarily from Spain and Oriental countries.

Each group had its own rabbinic leadership. The traditions are, therefore, different in some aspects. For example, Ashkenazic Jews outlawed multiple wives in the 11th century, while the Sephardic Jews only recently outlawed this practice.

While traditions may differ concerning the actual observance, each of the feasts that we will study has a distinct purpose. They are not man-made holidays as we think of Thanksgiving or Independence Day. These holidays, or feasts, are significant in that they were set up by God, Himself. It can be difficult to find actual traditions and customs in the Bible. However, there are many stories that are illustrations or examples of them. If we know what the actual tradition or culture of the day was, the stories and lessons have deeper meaning.

In order for you to familiarize yourself with these illustrations, we've included questions based on scripture references you will be asked to read. Maybe some of these passages you've read or heard since early childhood Bible classes, but we will try to bring to your attention the culture that was happening in the background as these stories took place. Hopefully, you will gain some new insight from these familiar passages as you delve into understanding the behind-the-scenes traditions that underlie the stories.

And believe it or not, we've had people ask us, "Jesus wasn't really Jewish, was He?" Well, just to set the record straight, Jesus was born Jewish and in his life kept the entire Jewish law. He may not have worn a yarmulke (kippah—skullcap), though. While Exodus 28:4 mentions a head covering for the priests, there is no clear answer for when the general population of Jewish men began wearing a yarmulke. However, in Chapter 4 of this book, we'll learn about some clothing typical for

Jewish men during Jesus' time. In Matthew 1 and Luke 3, we find His heritage followed both through Mary and Joseph to be a descendant of the tribe of Judah, more specifically through King David, the root of Jesse. He fulfilled all of the prophecies of the Bible regarding the first coming of the Jewish Messiah. He died as a Jew and was resurrected as a Jew. He never converted to anything. He will return as a Jewish bridegroom to "steal away" his bride (believers in Jesus). And, we, His people, are going to live for eternity with a Jewish kinsman-redeemer, Yeshua (Jesus).

It is unfortunate that the Christian church has so little knowledge of our Jewish roots. It is, after all, the origin of Christianity. The early "Christian church" was completely Jewish. They were Jews who realized that their long-awaited Messiah had come in the person of Jesus. The Church today is the opposite; we are almost all Gentiles, and we have lost the heritage of the Jewish roots of Christianity.

After hearing a presentation on the Passover, we realized how little we knew about the Jewish religion. We considered that spending time getting to know some of the customs and culture of our Jewish Savior might allow us to know Him better. And, indeed, among simple verses that we had been familiar with since childhood Bible story days, we found deeper understanding. The information was so new, fresh, and exciting to us that we began studying and sharing what we were learning. The more we learned, the deeper we fell in love with the Messiah and the intricacies of God's word. God has orchestrated a series of events in our lives that have given us a great appreciation for the Jewish people. The more we have learned, the more strongly we believe that Israel and the Jews are still important to God and to us in today's world. So, here we are: Gentiles teaching Jewish tradition!

Consider Genesis 12:1-3:

> *"NOW the LORD said to Abram,'Go forth from your country, and from your relatives, and from your father's house, to the land which I will show you; and I will make you a great nation, and I will bless you, and make your name*

> *great; and so you shall be a blessing; and I will bless those who bless you, and the one who curses you I will curse. And in you all the families of the earth shall be blessed.'"*

This promise from God to Abram has not been revoked. The details of God's word are not a coincidence. Today, Jews validate Jesus as Messiah by the customs and feasts they still keep, because the feasts were set up to point to the Christ, and Jesus fulfilled every aspect of these feasts. These traditional feasts of the Jews have as much to offer to Gentile believers in Jesus (Yeshua) as they do to Jews. God set up the feast days for the nation of Israel to follow. These special days were not just randomly picked by a person or government; they were appointed by God. It seems quite appropriate for Gentile Christians, then, to examine more closely the festivals and days that God thought were important.

Many people today dismiss these Jewish feasts because the feasts are Jewish. Yes, they are Jewish feasts, but more importantly, they are Biblical feasts. And, Jews today are proclaiming God's plan of salvation by keeping their feast days and Sabbaths, even though most do not believe that Jesus is the Messiah.

Some churches teach that it is wrong to have anything to do with the Jewish feasts. They base this on our freedom in Christ and on the following scripture, Galatians 4: 9-11, which says:

> *"But now that you have come to know God, or rather to be known by God, how is it that you turn back again to the weak and worthless elemental things, to which you desire to be enslaved all over again? You observe days and months and seasons and years. I fear for you, that perhaps I have labored over you in vain."*

The problem that the author of Galatians, Paul, was addressing was that Galatians were putting their trust in keeping the feasts and the law, trying to justify their salvation through the Mosaic Law rather than through grace. They were trying to complete good works to merit salvation. Paul essentially asks them why they would want to put themselves back under legalism since the Messiah freed them from trying to earn their salvation. This verse, taken in context, is addressing a primarily Gentile audience, not necessarily a Jewish audience. It does not tell Jews to quit keeping Jewish feasts. One could just as easily argue that this should prevent Christians from celebrating Christmas or Easter. The point of the verse is that observation of special days does not make a person righteous before God, but that the blood of Jesus makes one righteous.

In this study, we are not advocating one way or the other about observing the feasts. We have celebrated them in our home some years, and some years not, but we always learn something new from them. The Bible gives us some insight as to the usefulness of studying the feasts. Colossians 2:16 says, "Therefore let no one act as your judge in regard to food or drink or in respect to a festival or a new moon or a Sabbath day — things which are a mere shadow of what is to come; but the substance belongs to Christ." This verse tells us the real purpose for the feasts; the feasts were intended to show us the Messiah.

Only an actual, existent object and one that is relatively close to a light will cast a shadow. Jesus was in the beginning with the Father (John 1:1). He casts a shadow throughout the entire Old Testament and into the New Testament where, finally, the person of Jesus, who is casting the shadow, is revealed.

These feasts that were set up for the Israelites to observe are not an afterthought. God did not just randomly pick some days for the purpose of giving the people a day off from work. From the beginning, they were set up to teach about God's plan for the redemption of man. The festival days are ultimately fulfilled in Christ. This verse also teaches us a truth about our freedom in Christ. If someone chooses to celebrate one of these feasts, then we have no right to judge him on that issue. If you desire further study, Romans 14 has much more to say concerning this idea of judging one another dependent upon specifically chosen actions.

As we study these feasts, we are going to learn a lot about the Jewish religion. As we learn about their customs and laws, it is tempting to judge them for what appears to be blind legalism. Every time that we have this temptation, let's challenge ourselves, instead, to examine our own list of beliefs. The Christian church has a long history of adding things to the Gospel. Everything from church attendance, to good works, to not smoking or drinking has been added as a condition for salvation, in some instances.

We heard a story once about a group of American missionaries training with German missionaries preparing to enter Russia. The German missionaries were eager for a break in the meetings so that they could enjoy some ale, while the American missionaries were longing for some time out to smoke. However, each thought the other was committing a terrible sin during the break!

Churches have split, and people have stopped going to church over any number of insignificant details. We all have areas in our lives where we fulfill the letter of the law while ignoring the spirit of the law. We often appear holy to those around us, but we know in our hearts that we are not living a life for which Jesus would be proud.

Let's go through this study, then, with a humble heart, showing respect for the people God has chosen and the customs, feasts, and laws He gave them. God appointed the Jewish sacrificial system to direct people to the Messiah. Let's use this opportunity to remove obstacles from our own thinking and to draw closer to Him.

So, what are the feasts of Israel? The Israelites were given seven annual feasts as well as a weekly Sabbath. God commanded them to go to Jerusalem three times each year to celebrate these feasts. The first trip to Jerusalem was to celebrate the feasts of Passover, Unleavened Bread, and First Fruits. These three feasts happen in fairly rapid succession, and, grouped together, they are sometimes collectively called the Feast of Unleavened Bread. The second trip, 50 days later, celebrated the feast of Weeks (what most Gentile Christians know as Pentecost) and the last trip to Jerusalem was to observe the feasts of Trumpets, Day of Atonement, and Tabernacles (or Booths). These three feasts again occur relatively quickly, within the time span of about three weeks, and are sometimes collectively called the Feast of Tabernacles or Booths.

Deuteronomy 16:16-17 says, "Three times in a year all your males shall appear before the LORD your God in the place which He chooses, at the Feast of Unleavened Bread and at the Feast of Weeks and at the Feast of Booths, and they shall not appear before the LORD empty-handed. Every man shall give as he is able, according to the blessing of the LORD your God which He has given you."

FEAST OF UNLEAVENED BREAD				**FEAST OF WEEKS**
Passover (Pesach)	**Unleavened Bread (Matzah)**	**First Fruits**		**Weeks (Shavuot)**
1st Month 14th Day	1st Month 15th Day	The day after Sabbath, during the Week of Unleavened Bread. This also begins the Counting of the Omer.	50 days	Also known as Pentecost; The day after the 7th Sabbath following First Fruits

The feasts are grouped so that three trips to Jerusalem will allow the celebration of all seven feasts. Today's Jews do not go to Jerusalem three times each year with their sacrifices and offerings because there is no temple in which to make the sacrifice. Solomon's temple was destroyed in 586 B.C. by the Babylonians and King Nebuchadnezzar. Then, over 650 years later (tradition says on the same day, the ninth of Av), the Romans destroyed the rebuilt temple in 70 A.D. You can read about the rebuilding period in the Old Testament books of Nehemiah and Ezra. Because the temples were both destroyed many years apart, but both on the ninth of Av, Jewish people commemorate this day as Tishah B'av (literally translated, "the ninth of Av"). This Hebrew calendar month falls within the modern months of July and August.

For every interesting symbolism or custom we will highlight in this study, there are probably two or three more that could have been included. The history and traditions and culture of the Jewish people are rich with abundant opportunity to find Jesus in the Old Testament as well as the New Testament. This book is not intended to be an exhaustive account of all symbolisms and traditions for each of these feasts. But, we hope that God's word becomes wonderfully real and relevant in your life and that it influences your actions and thoughts as it has for us.

FEAST OF TABERNACLES (BOOTHS)

3-4 month period	**Trumpets (Rosh Hashanah)**	**10 Days of Awe**	**Day of Atonement (Yom Kippur)**	4 days	**Tabernacles or Booths (Sukkot)**	Shemini Atzeret (The assembly of the 8th day)
	7th Month 1st Day		7th Month 10th Day		7th Month 15th Day Lasts 7 days	

When we were in Kauai recently, we were reminded of the beauty of the water ritual in the Feast of Tabernacles and the significance of Jesus' statement to come to Him if anyone thirsts. We had hiked half of the day, four miles on beautiful but sometimes slippery trails, crossing back and forth over a little river. Not knowing exactly what we would find at the end of the hike caused us all to be a little skeptical of whether or not the trek was worth the effort. Then we began to hear the sound of something wonderful before we caught a glimpse of it. As we stepped out of the lush tropics, we stood in open-mouthed awe at the bottom of a 410-foot waterfall. It was hard to hear one another speak over the thundering sound of the falling water. The beauty was beyond description, and the water was cold and refreshing.

We ventured into the pool at the base of the falls, eager to experience everything about the alluring power of the water. We felt pricked and stung as if by needles as we swam under it, irritated as it splashed and sprayed us while we stood behind it. But when we lay floating on our backs, our heads resting in the pool looking up at the waterfall, we were surrounded by a luxuriant green mountainside; birds floated in the sky far above; and muted, calming sounds of underwater peace enveloped us. Every droplet glimmered and danced, celebrating its wildly passionate plunge into our little pool of paradise.

The surprising beauty of that waterfall experience which God had prepared at the end of our trek is an exquisite foretaste of the life-giving water ritual and its significance that we will learn about in Chapter 8: The Feast of Tabernacles. It was a cherished gift from our Heavenly Father that reminded us of how God fulfills the thirst of our parched hearts. During that experience in the waterfall, we were also acutely aware of how God spares no effort in showing us His amazing creativity and beauty. With such a loving Creator reaching out to us, and with us being given so many rich opportunities to see Him in His creation and in His written revelation, our purpose in writing this study is that we can share how we have learned to trust Him increasingly with every aspect of our lives.

So we invite you to dive in to God's word with us as we proceed to look into the feasts of the Jewish faith, celebrated for centuries before Christianity even came into being. First Peter 1:10-12 says,

> *"As to this salvation, the prophets who prophesied of the grace that would come to you made careful search and inquiry, seeking to know what person or time the Spirit of Christ within them was indicating as He predicted the sufferings of Christ and the glories to follow. It was revealed to them that they were not serving themselves, but you, in these things which now have been announced to you through those who preached the gospel to you by the Holy Spirit sent from heaven — things into which angels long to look."*

God's word and His prophecies have withstood the element of time, surviving throughout generations to reach us. They are still powerful and applicable. All of the prophets' sacrifices, all of their questioning and investigating and all of their careful inquiry were endured for the purpose of bringing us truth. It's overwhelming, really. God's word was meant for Jews and Gentiles alike! What can we glean from the prophets and traditions of old? What customs and culture will we pass on to future generations from our understanding and practice of God's word that will affect the eternal souls of many? Listen for the shofar of your soul at the Feast of Trumpets, and feel the untamed wind of the Holy Spirit at Pentecost. Amidst the chaos of your life experience, rest during Shabbat. Draw near to God's word and enjoy a feast of faith!

CHAPTER ONE

SABBATH
(Shabbat)

— *A Lesson on Rest*

With 3.2 miles left of the 26.2-mile marathon, Dallas wanted to quit. Four months of training in wind and cold, sacrificing time to make the long runs, icing down painful knees, and sticking to the training when it got tough brought her to this point in the marathon, and here she was, more than willing to give it all up with only three miles to go. Carl had slowed behind her, and she wasn't sure how far back he was. "I didn't just want to stop running, I wanted to lie down right in the middle of the road and declare defeat!" she admits. The curb was at least a step or two away. "I could at least walk over to the curb," she thought. "But, it's so far over there!" Several miles back, she'd already learned, as many runners do during a marathon, that walking hurt just as much or worse than running (if you could call what she was still doing at this point running).

"Yes, quitting right here in the middle of the road would do quite nicely. I just need rest," she thought. However, in those moments of wrestling with herself about how many people would trip over her if she would just lie down in the road and give up, she realized she had made it about three more feet. In fact, if she put her head down and just tried to make it the two steps that she could see before her visor got in the way, she could probably make it just about three feet worth of pavement. And so, for the next three miles, that's exactly what she did: She put her head down, took two little, gimpy steps, and checked off three more feet of pavement. "I lifted my head once, just a tad, only to see a small hill ahead. Quick as I could, I returned to my three feet of pavement, which had somehow become almost comfortable in a weird sort of way," she says.

There's one great thing about focusing on only three feet of pavement: You can't really tell if you're going uphill or not in such a small space, so you can't worry about what's ahead. We all find ourselves living life this way occasionally, trying to just survive the moment. When looking ahead to the future brings into focus only more daunting hills to climb, we have to put our head back down, focus our mind on the present moment, and endure to the end. Sometimes rest must wait until our journey or task is complete, and other times we need to creatively find a way to rest within the agony of the journey.

PHYSICAL REST

The God of the Universe, in His great wisdom, saw the need for our frail human bodies to have rest. Leviticus 23 tells us that God wanted the nation of Israel to rest on the Sabbath:

> *THE LORD spoke again to Moses, saying, "Speak to the sons of Israel, and say to them, 'The LORD'S appointed times which you shall proclaim as holy convocations - My appointed times are these: 'For six days work may be done; but on the seventh day there is a Sabbath of complete rest, a holy convocation. You shall not do any work; it is a Sabbath to the LORD in all your dwellings.'"*

Sabbath (or Shabbat, the Hebrew word for rest) occurs on the seventh day. Some Christian churches call Sunday "the Christian Sabbath," or they believe that Jesus changed the Sabbath to Sunday. This is not correct. The Bible never calls Sunday anything except the first day of the week. As the Jews see it, only the Sabbath has a name, all other days are numbered, and this makes the Sabbath the focal point of the week.

God tells the Israelites to work for six days and then rest on the seventh. God repeats this command in Exodus 20, with the giving of the Ten Commandments. Exodus 20:8-11 says this about the Sabbath:

> *Remember the Sabbath day, to keep it holy. Six days you shall labor and do all your work, but the seventh day is a Sabbath of the LORD your God; in it you shall not do any work, you or your son or your daughter, your male or your female servant or your cattle or your sojourner who stays with you. For in six days the LORD made the heavens and the earth, the sea and all that is in them, and rested on the seventh day; therefore the LORD blessed the Sabbath day and made it holy.*

The seventh day is a Sabbath of the Lord, or a "rest" of the Lord. God set this pattern for us in the story of creation. In Genesis, God worked for six days and rested on the seventh. The Sabbath day was fixed to be a perpetual reminder of God, our Creator, and our need to find rest in Him.

When God provided manna for the Israelites while in the desert, He provided a double portion on the sixth day of the week, so they would not have to collect any on Shabbat. In this way, He provided a way for them to rest.

The Jewish day starts at sundown and lasts until the following evening. This is based on wording of the creation account in Genesis 1:5, which said, "God called the light 'day,' and the darkness he called 'night.' And there was evening, and there was morning — the first day." Because it appears that God reckons time from evening to morning, Sabbath starts at sundown (eighteen minutes prior to sundown, to be exact) on Friday evening and continues until Saturday evening.

The Sabbath day starts (like most festival days do) with the lighting of candles and a blessing. Usually two candles, or sometimes one for every person present, are lit on Sabbath. Kindling a fire is considered work, and God commanded that no work be done on Sabbath; for this reason, the woman who lights the Sabbath candles then closes her eyes and says a blessing, "Blessed are you, oh Lord our God, King of the Universe who has sanctified us with His commandments and commanded us to kindle the Sabbath lights." Sabbath does not start until she opens her eyes. In this way, she did not break the Sabbath by kindling a fire. Sabbath candle-lighting times are published in some newspapers and on Jewish calendars to help people know exactly when to light the candles in their time zone. The candles mimic God's action on the first day of creation. He conquered darkness with light.

Read John 1:1-12.

1. How does John refer to Jesus in verses 4, 5, & 9?

____

____

After the candles are lit, it is traditional to greet others with "Shabbat shalom," or "Sabbath peace." The table is covered with a white tablecloth to remind the Jewish people that while they were wandering in the desert, manna covered the earth. They bake two loaves of challot (the plural form of challah, which is a white, egg-based bread) to remember that God provided a double portion of manna on the Sabbath. These two loaves also serve to remind them of the two rows of showbread that were in the temple. On Sabbath afternoon, there are adult classes in Torah and the study of the Talmud. (We will learn more about the Torah and the Talmud later in this study.)

While no work is allowed on the Sabbath, this prohibition against work has created some interesting rules and ways to fulfill the letter of the law that sometimes ignores the spirit of the law. Jewish people have a list of

39 things that cannot be done on the Sabbath. These include such things as building a fire, tearing, tying, and walking too far, among others.

The prohibition against building a fire has been expanded to include using any electronic equipment. If a person completes an electric circuit, that person has in effect kindled a fire. Therefore, you cannot drive a car, press a button on an elevator, or turn on a light switch. You can have a friendly Gentile (goy) do it for you, or you can turn the light on before Shabbat and leave it on for 24 hours. (Goy is the singular form of Goyim and means nation. Goyim, then, means nations.) The Ethiopian Jews historically have done without light on Shabbat. When they immigrated to Israel, their Ashkenazi brothers showed them ways to get around this prohibition. But the Ethiopian Jews replied, "We know how to get around the law; we are trying to keep the law." That statement can sure serve as a good motive check, can't it?

In order to not complete a circuit by requiring riders to push a button, elevators in Jewish hotels and buildings automatically stop on every floor (or every other floor in tall buildings) during Sabbath operation. All food preparation is completed before Shabbat, so that no cooking happens during this 24-hour period. Walking more than a "Sabbath's day walk" (3/4 mile from city limit or where you are spending Sabbath) from home is prohibited. This has proven to be too confining in modern times, so some modifications have been made. It is permissible to put a rope around an area, and it becomes "your home." This area is called an eruv. You can walk within this eruv any amount that you need without breaking the law. Over time, the eruvs continue to get bigger to accommodate more travel. For instance, the entire old city of Jerusalem is now an eruv.

It is prohibited to tear an object on Shabbat. It is even debated if it is lawful to tear toilet tissue. Since toilet paper is perforated, some argue that it is not work to tear a perforation. Modern-day Christians may see this as unreasonable legalism, but an observant Jew may be reminded of the distinction of the day and the holiness of the God he serves even in such an ordinary place as the bathroom (Greenberg, 1983).

When looked at from the Jewish point of view, we can gain a great appreciation for what a Sabbath day can do to build a family and to help them stay focused on God. Wouldn't it be great to have one day each week where you did not drive a car, watch TV, or use or turn on or off any electrical power? When we were growing up, our Sundays slightly resembled the Jewish observance of Sabbath. The malls and most of the stores were closed on Sundays, and there were no Little League sports games scheduled. We went to church, had lunch as a family, and played with all the kids on the block while our parents visited in the yard. Today, Sunday is another work day for many. Nearly all the stores are open, and we find ourselves racing out of church to make it on time to one of the kids' sporting events. Some weeks we have barely had time for lunch. We have four children, so over the years in which they were all at home, allowing each of them just one activity each kept us busy. During those years, we had to be very creative to carve out family time and rest time for them and for us. Even now, we long for the days of our childhood, when Sunday was more of a rest day spent with family and friends.

Jewish tradition personifies Shabbat, regarding Shabbat as a very important guest. All chores and preparations are completed before Shabbat, the honored guest, arrives. And what is not finished is set aside until the guest leaves. They also have a ritual to say good-bye to Shabbat. Sabbath ends when three stars are visible on Saturday night. One tradition is to go for a "star hunt," a walk to look for stars. As Sabbath started 18 minutes before sundown on Friday evening, it ends 42 minutes after sundown on Saturday evening. What a sweet treat; Sabbath is 25 hours long! Who doesn't want a rest day with an extra hour?

At the close of Sabbath, it's back to work. The first work is to start a fire. A braided candle with multiple wicks called the havdalah candle is lit. "Havdalah" means "separate." This is a ceremony of separation or of "saying good-bye" to the Sabbath. It is a reminder that Shabbat is separated or set apart from the rest of the week.

A havdalah cup of wine is filled, literally, to overflowing as an expression that the coming week will be filled with goodness to abundance.

The flame of the havdalah candle is put out in the wine that spills over into a tray to remind them that some of the holiness of Sabbath will last throughout the week. Citrus-y, fragrant spices are passed around for everyone to enjoy and to remember the sweet aroma of Shabbat.

Read the following passages: 2 Corinthians 2:14-15 and John 10:10.

2. How does Jesus fulfill the symbolisms of Shabbat?

____

____

In the marathon, when Dallas so longed to quit, but then she decided to single-mindedly focus on the three feet of pavement in front of her, it was with some amount of surprise that she began to sense the finish line might be near. She peeked past her visor's edge, and sure enough, about 200 meters away was the finish line, all decked out with balloons and swarming with people. Where had all these people come from? They were cheering and clapping, and a band was playing. In fact, there were people all around her running the same race; Carl had caught up and was running along beside her. How long had he been there? She had vaguely thought about him back at mile 23 when she had chosen to enter her three-feet-of-pavement "rest," but he was lagging behind. Now that he had caught up, what a difference it made to have someone to run with!

We held up our heads, put smiles on our faces, and tried our best "I'm a runner!" form. While our heads did indeed stay up and smiles came to our faces, there was absolutely no response from our bodies except the pitiful little gimpy jog that had carried us the last three miles, three feet of pavement at a time. With a few steps of the race left, we reached for each other's hands, and we lifted our arms in triumph as we crossed the finish! Now we could enjoy some *rest, sweet rest!*

God had a clear finish line all along and waited to rejoice with us. He had been there in the beginning when we started the journey. He brought people along to enjoy the adventure together and cheer us on. And when we lost sight of that, reduced to just three feet of pavement out of fear and pain and exhaustion, He was there too, offering rest, applauding us on.

MENTAL REST

In Isaiah 58:13-14, we catch a glimpse of what God had in mind for the Sabbath:

> *If because of the Sabbath, you turn your foot from doing your own pleasure on* My *holy day, and call the Sabbath a delight, the holy day of the* LORD *honorable, and shall*

> *honor it, desisting from your own ways, from seeking your own pleasure, and speaking your own word, then you will take delight in the LORD, and I will make you ride on the heights of the earth; and I will feed you with the heritage of Jacob your father, for the mouth of the LORD has spoken.*

Observant Jews today enjoy the Sabbath as a restful, joyous time with family and an opportunity to study the Torah. God has made a day for us to stop thinking about ourselves and take delight in Him! Every other day is often filled with our selfish desires and intents; we can at least take one day to focus on Him and His will.

At some point, the focus seems to have changed into keeping the law, not seeking God. For instance, the Jewish leaders argued that writing just two letters or weaving two threads was breaking the Sabbath. Let's look at God's response to a people who keep his law outwardly but inwardly are far from Him. Isaiah 1:13-14 says, "Stop bringing meaningless offerings! Your incense is detestable to me. New Moons, Sabbaths and convocations — I cannot bear your evil assemblies. Your New Moon festivals and your appointed feasts my soul hates. They have become a burden to me; I am weary of bearing them" (NIV).

The Jewish leaders had become focused on fulfilling man-made laws concerning the Sabbath, so it is easy to see why they had conflicts with the teachings and actions of Jesus. Jesus understood God's purpose for the Sabbath, as shown in Matthew 12.

Read Matthew 12:1-14.

1. What did Jesus do on the Sabbath that was considered unlawful?

____

____

2. What was His argument to defend Himself?

____

____

3. Demonstrating the seriousness of this perceived offense, what did the Pharisees plan to do to Jesus?

____

____

In Mark 2:27-28, Jesus is speaking: "And He was saying to them, 'The Sabbath was made for man, and not man for the Sabbath. Consequently, the Son of Man is Lord even of the Sabbath.'"

4. Using these passages, also refer to Luke 11:46. What observations can you make about the hearts of the Pharisees?

____

____

5. What do you think was God's intent for the Sabbath?

____

____

The Sabbath was made for us. We all need to rest from work occasionally. We can get so caught up in doing the work, and many of us forget to enjoy the ride. We (Dallas and Carl) bought a tandem bike recently. These bicycles are also frequently called "divorce machines." We prefer to tell people, "Wherever your marriage is headed, you'll get there faster on a tandem." Carl rides in the front in the "captain" position, while Dallas rides in the back as the "stoker." We have to admit, though, our first few rides weren't very pretty.

Dallas had a lot of "suggestions" concerning the driving. She kept leaning out to the side trying to see where we were headed, which of course, unbalanced the bike, causing Carl to have to overcorrect the steering. After owning the tandem for only a few days, on a day while Carl was at work, our youngest son, Cooper, wanted to ride the new bike. Dallas agreed to ride as the captain, allowing him to be the stoker. Being just eight years old, our son was accustomed to being along for the ride with no responsibility or authority to affect the final destination. He just sat on the back and pedaled away ... no complaints, no questions, and no "suggestions." Amazing what you can learn from an eight-year-old stoker!

When we look ahead, trying to control where we are going, it upsets God's balance for our lives. When we try to take over someone else's job or compare our gifts and skill sets with someone else rather than resting in the job we've been given, it creates conflict and hinders our journey. Dallas is learning to rest in God's authority, to be at peace with where He's taking her. On the bike, she only occasionally fights the urge to lean out and see where we are going. It's much more fun for both of us to just pedal along and enjoy the ride. We've logged quite a few miles on our tandem, even completing a 100-mile race. But now, Dallas starts almost every ride with, "I'm just following you, 'O Captain! My Captain!'"

Our minds need rest from doing all the work of navigating this life, just like our physical bodies do. Read Hebrews 4:1-11. As you read, note all the uses of the word "rest."

6. Considering this passage, why do you think Gentile Christians do not observe the Sabbath, even though keeping it is one of the Ten Commandments?

____

Read Matthew 11:28-30.

7. What do you think it means "to enter His rest"?

____

8. If Jesus' yoke wasn't the study of Torah, what was it, and why did Jesus say it is easy?

____

We can see through these passages that the Sabbath has its fulfillment in Christ. He is our rest. We can keep this commandment by knowing Yeshua and the rest we have in Him. Jesus died for our sins, and only his death pays the price for sins. We need to rest from the work of trying to save ourselves, and we need to have faith in His work. And, we don't have to wait for just one day each week to experience rest. We have rest in the Messiah every day, anytime. He has a standing appointment with us. He is our light, our rest, our provision.

Rabbis in Jesus' day would take students under their tutelage. The "yoke" of the Rabbi was the Torah. It was considered to be a great burden to the student to learn, memorize, study, and become obedient to the Torah. However, Jesus introduced a new concept of learning through His gentleness, through His humility, and through teaching us to model our lives after Him. He shares our burdens, allowing us to find rest for our weary souls.

Our daughter, Paris, and son, Connor, both ran on the cross-country team at their high school, and our family has been to many of their meets to cheer for them. The different teams often wear t-shirts with inspirational sayings on the back. Well, maybe "inspirational" isn't quite the word for some of them. "My sport is your sport's punishment" isn't one that necessarily inspires us to sign up for their team! However, one of our favorite slogans from these shirts is "Cross-country is 10% physical and 90% mental." Our minds have so much to do with how we act and with what we choose to believe. Our minds need rest. When the children were little, Carl was in medical school and residency. His hours away from home were long, sometimes 36 hours at a time. Dallas would yearn for a rest away from the kids. It wasn't the children or all their physical needs she needed a break from, it was a relief from the responsibility, a rest for her mind.

Rest comes in many forms and when we allow the Lord to come along beside us, sharing our yoke, we are able to find rest amidst the distress of the journey. We can then share this rest, serving others as we act as the hands and feet of Jesus — sharing their burdens, encouraging them on, providing creative moments of rest. Recently, Carl chose to run a half-marathon with our son, Carson. Dallas opted out, but positioned herself on a lonely stretch of the race course. In fact, there was no one else cheering that she could see in either direction. She began to notice a difference in the runners as they realized she was there. If they noticed her, their form would change just a bit, a little more bounce in their step until they passed her. If she cheered for them, their head would lift, their countenance would change, and maybe even a smile would cross their face. For those few moments, their minds rested from the pain.

What if we are the only one cheering on a friend in this life's race, the only one offering an opportunity for rest in the Messiah? Let's don't miss out on the rest God offers us. Our hope isn't in getting through the tough time, but in knowing more intimately the One who is running with us in it. He is the only hope for rest from the pain. Our part is resting in His will for our lives, allowing Him to be our "Captain."

Take in what Ezekiel 20:11-12 says:

> *And I gave them My statutes and informed them of My ordinances, by which, if a man observes them, he will live. And also I gave them My Sabbaths to be a sign between Me and them, that they might know that I am the LORD who sanctifies them.*

As far as we know, only one person has kept all the statutes and ordinances God gave. He lived — not just until He was crucified, but death itself could not keep him in the grave! And, through Him, Yeshua, we have life also. The Sabbath still stands, however, as a sign between the Lord and His people. In fact, it has been said that "more than the Jews have kept Shabbat, Shabbat has kept the Jews."

We were privileged to visit Europe recently. We toured several synagogues in the city of Prague in the Czech Republic, including the Pinkas synagogue in the old Jewish quarter. The names of over 77,000 Bohemian and Moravian Jews who lost their lives in the Holocaust of World War II are written on the walls of this synagogue. In 1933, before World War II, the population of Jews in Czechoslovakia (currently two separate countries, the Czech Republic and Slovakia) was about 357,000. Today, these two countries together have only about 6,500 Jews (Mishory, 2010). As we traveled on to Budapest, Hungary, we learned that nearly half of the Jewish population there died in the Holocaust.

After Budapest, we continued to Poland, touring the site of the concentration camps of Auschwitz-Birkenau. We were profoundly touched at the sights of the crematoriums, the vacant barracks, the barbed wire fencing, the massive amounts of clothing, shoes, and human hair — a testimony to the more than two million Jewish lives destroyed there. We will forever be changed simply by our visit to this concentration camp. However, the sight that most impressed us, the scene still vividly clear in our minds, was the group of uniformed Israeli soldiers against the backdrop of this death camp, respectfully touring it with us — a living testimony to the fulfillment of God's word. Out of the hatred and death of the holocaust was re-born a nation: Israel, the only homeland for the Jewish people, complete with soldiers willing to die for her — a modern reality that was foretold in ages past (Jeremiah 32:37-42).

In light of all the destruction and horror the European Jews went through, how did they survive? How did this enormous attempt at their destruction fail? Jeremiah 31:35-36 answers it best:

> *"Thus says the Lord,*
> *Who gives the sun for light by day,*
> *And the fixed order of the moon and the stars for light by night,*
> *Who stirs up the sea so that its waves roar;*
> *The Lord of hosts is His name:*
> *'If this fixed order departs*
> *From before Me,' declares the Lord,*
> *'Then the offspring of Israel also shall cease*
> *From being a nation before Me forever.'"*

While the Holocaust of World War II is the most recent grand scale attempt, many other endeavors to annihilate the Jewish people have been made throughout history. We'll learn about one of these in the chapter on Purim. However, God has preserved the Jewish people, and part of that plan has undoubtedly included keeping the Sabbath. Essentially, this act of setting time apart each week for rest, for family, and for building traditions based on God has helped to sustain the Jewish culture. This tradition endured through their dispersions from Israel and served to keep the Jews as a distinct people group. Indeed, while "the Jews have kept Shabbat, Shabbat has kept the Jews."

What are some traditions you are doing or you could begin in your family to encourage some God-focused time?

____

____

Dallas was recently asked to volunteer in the three-year-old classroom at church. The children were learning about having a quiet time. The teacher asked them to lie down on little blankets in the floor to pray quietly to God. Dallas chose to lie down also and found that it's quite dangerous to have a quiet time with ten three-year olds! Little western-boot-clad feet lashed out at her head, tiny ponytails bobbed restlessly up and down on one of her legs, while miniature black patent shoes kicked out a rhythm against the other. She couldn't help but think, "Is this me, God?" It is so easy to be like these easily distracted children during our own quiet times. In our attempts to have a quiet rest alone with the Lord, are we lashing out at God for the perceived problems in our lives, restlessly bouncing between prayer and the to-do list, kicking out a tantrum over unanswered prayers?

In our busy, loud, demanding world, Shabbat cries out to us, "Rest." And just like the greeting of the day, "Shabbat shalom," peace follows. Jesus, be our rest, our peace. Here is what God's word urges us, translated into modern English:

> *God keeps renewing the promise and setting the date as today, just as He did in David's psalm, centuries later than the original invitation: Today, please listen, don't turn a deaf ear… And so this is still a live promise. It wasn't canceled at the time of Joshua; otherwise, God wouldn't keep renewing the appointment for "today." The promise of "arrival" and "rest" is still available for God's people. God Himself is at rest. And at the end of the journey we'll surely rest with God. So let's keep at it and eventually arrive at the place of rest, not drop out through some sort of disobedience. God means what He says. What He says goes. His powerful Word is sharp as a surgeon's scalpel, cutting through everything, whether doubt or defense, laying us open to listen and obey. Nothing and no one is impervious to God's Word. We can't get away from it — no matter what. Now that we know what we have — Jesus, this great High Priest with ready access to God — let's not let it slip through our fingers. We don't have a priest who is out of touch with our reality. He's been through weakness and testing, experienced it all — all but the sin. So let's walk right up to Him and get what He is so ready to give. Take the mercy; accept the help* (Hebrews 4:7-15, The Message).

Shabbat shalom!

CHAPTER TWO

PASSOVER
(Pesach)

— *A Lesson on Passionate Love*

Ava narrowly escaped everyone's notice as she slipped out of the house. She was wearing her best shoes with her everyday school dress, but thankfully no one stopped her to ask what on earth she was doing. Frantically wondering where she could discard the simple school dress for her best Sunday dress she wore beneath it, she ran for the train to meet her school teacher. On the way, she pulled the school frock over her head and tossed it behind a large tree at the edge of the road. Finally arriving breathless at the train station, she caught up with her teacher, Roy, who was waiting for her. The two of them headed to Roy's uncle's house in the next town for a secret wedding — their own! It was 1917, and Ava was only 14!

After vowing their lives to one another in marriage, they boarded the train to return home. When Ava's parents heard the news of this scandalous wedding, they threatened to have the marriage annulled. However, Ava solemnly promised she would run away at the first opportunity and wed Roy again. Ava's father reluctantly gave his blessing to their union, and so, Ava and Roy remained happily married.

Their sweet marriage was not, however, without adversity. Their first son died of pneumonia when he was only six weeks old. Their second son was born with a cleft palate and cleft lip, requiring numerous surgeries during the years of the Great Depression. Moves and career changes, financial hardships and wars tried their marriage, but they faithfully served the Lord and each other for 55 years, until a sudden heart attack claimed Roy's life. Ava remained a widow for the next 14 years, outliving her only surviving son, who was Dallas' father.

Ava always enjoyed telling her grandchildren, including Dallas, the story of her anxious flight from home and the exciting train ride on the morning of her secret wedding. The retelling of the story frequently included a giggle, and with a mischievous look in her eye, she would say the sustaining ingredient in her marriage relationship was love, a passionate love that defied traditional culture, dared to risk, defended vows, and endured time and tragedy.

A PASSIONATE LOVE SAVES FROM DEATH

God displays a passionate love for all of His people throughout His word and throughout history. It is a love that goes against popular societal views. It is a love that is willing to take risks. In fact, He loved us so much that He gave His to Son to die for us. In the Old Testament, He set up a series of feasts to help a nation of people remember that He loved them so passionately, He delivered them from certain death. In the upcoming section, we will be studying the feast of Passover: God's appointed commemoration of His passionate love for His people.

Passover is the first of seven annual feasts of Israel. It celebrates the Hebrews' freedom from captivity in Egypt. The Hebrews had been slaves in Egypt for about 430 years when God sent Moses to deliver them. While Moses pleaded with Pharaoh to let the people go, Pharaoh refused. God began to send forth various plagues on the people and on the land, culminating with the 10th and final plague of the death of the firstborn people and animals throughout the land of Egypt. The Hebrews were given explicit instructions by God so that, if followed, the angel of death would not kill their firstborn, but instead, would pass over them. We would like to encourage you to take a few moments and read this account of Hebrew history, beginning back in Exodus 4 and continuing through Chapter 12 with the nation's miraculous escape through the Red Sea.

Having saved a whole nation from slavery and captivity, God wanted the people to remember this amazing act of deliverance and love. He instituted a feast to be observed yearly, for all generations, for the purpose of remembering this moment in their history. More importantly, Passover also pointed to a future Messiah who would free all people for all time from the slavery and bondage of sin. As we learn about Passover and as you consider God's word, be encouraged that while God was providing freedom from bondage for the Israelites, He was also passionately thinking about you.

Read the account of the first Passover in Exodus 12:1-51.

1. On what day were they to choose the lamb (v. 3)?

____

2. What was special about the lamb (v. 5)?

____

____

The Jewish family separated the sacrificial lamb from the others and watched it for four days between the 10th and 14th of Nisan to ensure it was unblemished and worthy to be sacrificed. They surely became somewhat attached to it during this time, making the sacrifice more painful. At the appointed time in history, on the very day that the Jewish people were choosing lambs from their flocks to be their sacrifices for their annual Passover celebration, the crowds were chanting to the ultimate Lamb of God, Jesus, as he entered the city of Jerusalem just days before his death, "Blessed is the King who comes in the name of the Lord; Peace in heaven and glory in the highest" (Luke 19:37-38)! In our Christian traditions, we know this day as Palm Sunday.

At that unforgettable Passover, the Jewish people were bringing their little lambs right up into their back yards, so to speak, just as Jesus was riding right into the temple courtyard. During these four days that Jesus was in Jerusalem, He endured some of the most serious questioning of His ministry by the religious leaders (Mark 11:1-14:11). He was, in fact, proving he was the perfect Lamb of God, without blemish, and worthy to be the sacrifice, the promised Messiah, for all people of all time. While tradition required the Jewish family to become close to their little sacrificial lamb by keeping it nearby and maintaining a watchful eye on it, in a similar way, we can become more attached to Jesus by spending time with Him in His word.

Record a time when you've been blessed by spending time with the perfect Lamb of God.

____

____

____

3. What were the Israelites doing with their sheep on the 14th day of Nissan (see Exodus 12:6)?

____

4. Read 1 Peter 1:18-19 and John 19:32-36 with Exodus 12:5 and 12:46. What words used to describe Jesus were also used to describe the lamb that was to be sacrificed?

____

____

God's holiness demands that He judge sin, and the price is costly. However, He provides a way of redemption. Jesus paid a great price for our redemption. He Himself was our sacrifice. He is the perfect Lamb of God.

5. From Exodus 12:7, 22, what were the Israelites supposed to do with the lamb's blood?

____

6. How were they to eat the lamb (vv. 11, 46)?

____

____

7. Why is this feast called Passover (v. 13)?

____

____

8. According to verses 13 and 23, what did the Lord have to "see" in order to pass over the door?

____

9. What do you think God has to "see" on us in order for death to "pass over" us (1 John 1:7 and Hebrews 9:11-14)?

____

10. What would happen to one outside the door (Ex. 12:22-23, 29-30)?

____

Just as a firstborn sheltered behind the door was saved from death, we can be saved by a "door" as well. In John 10:7-10, Jesus referred to Himself as a "door" or a "gate" for the sheep. He says in verses 9-10, "I am the door; if anyone enters through Me, he shall be saved, and shall go in and out, and find pasture. The thief comes only to steal, and kill, and destroy; I came that they might have life, and might have it abundantly." Jesus was speaking to a Jewish audience. Every year, they put the sacrificed blood of the lamb on their door at Passover, remembering that those outside the door were subject to God's judgment. As Christians, we understand that Jesus not only provided His blood for the sacrifice, but He is also our protective door delivering us from the judgment of death.

It is interesting to note here that the whole assembly took part in killing the lamb for Passover. Exodus 12:6 says, "… then the whole assembly of the congregation of Israel is to kill it at twilight." God's word is so amazing in that not a single detail is overlooked. Jesus, being the Passover Lamb, was killed by the whole assembly. From John 19:5-15, Luke 23:23, and Matthew 27:22-26, we read the accounts of Jesus before Pilate. Indeed, the whole assembly was involved in sacrificing the Lamb, including priests, Pharisees, common Jewish people, and even the Gentiles represented by Pilate and the Roman centurions. All of us have sinned. The Lamb of God was sacrificed so we can all have forgiveness and freedom from sin, and so the angel of death would pass over us. We are all in need of a Savior, we all need forgiveness, and each of us who have called on the name of the Lord Jesus Christ has been passed over by death and given new life for all eternity.

A PASSIONATE LOVE ADORES THOSE FAR OFF

While the whole assembly was responsible for the sacrifice of the lamb, they were not all allowed to take part in the Passover meal.

1. Who could and who could not celebrate the Passover meal (Exodus 12:43-51)?

Could:	Could not:
____________________	____________________
____________________	____________________
____________________	____________________

2. Read Romans 3:21-30.

From the phrase, "but now apart from the Law," who do you think can be included in having their sins "passed over" (v. 29)?

____

____

Why?

____

Basically, we learn from these verses in Exodus that those who desired to observe Passover didn't necessarily have to be from the nation of Israel, but they did have to be circumcised. Circumcision was established for the Israelites by God in Genesis 17 as a sign of His everlasting covenant to be their God throughout all generations. Every male among them was circumcised when he was eight days old as an outward sign of this covenant. Those who were not circumcised or were not a part of the nation of Israel were strangers, or foreigners, or sometimes referred to as "those who were far off."

We love seeing the phrase "those who were far off" anywhere in the Bible because we know it is talking about us. We did not live during the time of that first Passover. We do not have a Jewish heritage. We have only vague ideas of what the Jewish law requires and no idea how to keep it all! We are truly the ones "who are far off." Nevertheless, God was thinking of us and providing a way for us to know Him thousands of years before we were born ... even as He was setting up laws for the Israelites.

Ephesians 2:11-19 says that God was making a way for us Gentiles to become part of his family, which formerly was limited to the Jewish nation, long before we were even aware of our need for peace with God:

> *Therefore remember that formerly you, the Gentiles in the flesh, who are called "Uncircumcision" by the so-called "Circumcision," which is performed in the flesh by human hands — remember that you were at that time separate from Christ, excluded from the commonwealth of Israel, and strangers to the covenants of promise, having no hope and without God in the world. But now in Christ Jesus you who formerly were far off have been brought near by the blood of Christ. ... and He came and preached peace to you who were far away, and peace to those who were near; for through Him we both have our access in one Spirit to the*

> *Father. So then you are no longer strangers and aliens, but you are fellow citizens with the saints, and are of God's household ...."*

Oh, how thankful we are that God provided a way for us, strangers who were far off, to partake in the freedom of the Passover Lamb!

From the time of the Exodus from Egypt, Israel had been sacrificing a lamb every year and remembering that the blood of that lamb saved them from death and freed them from bondage.

3. Since Jesus is the Lamb of God, what does His sacrifice mean personally for you?

____

____

In John 1:29, John the Baptist calls Jesus, "the Lamb of God who takes away the sin of the world!" It seems more fitting to say that Jesus would be the Lamb of God to take away the sin of the Jews. It was, after all, the Jews who were looking for a messiah. The world was not even aware it needed a Savior. But, once again, God provided for everyone: the circumcised and the uncircumcised, the slave and the freeman, the whole congregation of Israel, the foreigner and the sojourner, and the ones who are far off. "But as many as received Him, to them He gave the right to become children of God, even to those who believe in His name" (John 1:12). Yes, even you and me. Indeed, John the Baptist said it correctly:

> *"Behold, the Lamb of God who takes away the sin of the WORLD!"*

God so passionately loves us that He gave His Son, the Lamb of God, to be a sacrifice on our behalf. The Lamb's blood guards the door of our heart, causing the angel of death to pass over us. As a result, we have everlasting life and complete freedom in Jesus the Messiah from the bondage of sin. No matter what personal sin has entangled us, we have complete freedom from it. Galatians 5:1 encourages us, "It was for freedom that Christ set us free; therefore, keep standing firm and do not be subject again to a yoke of slavery."

A PASSIONATE LOVE BLESSES

Psalm 32:1 is so true, "How blessed is he whose transgression is forgiven, whose sin is covered!" However, before the Messiah came, the Israelites did not have the luxury of freedom from sin for all time. Continual sacrifices had to be made on their behalf. Because God's laws for Israel depended on a system of animal sacrifice, it was imperative that there be a high priest to make the sacrifice. The priests had to be sanctified for the job of offering sacrifices at the temple. Sanctification means "to be made clean," or to be in "a state of purity," or to be "set apart." Leviticus 21:17-23 goes into quite some detail about priests who had any type of defect. Those who did were not able to "go into the veil or come near the altar." We will discuss the priests more in the Day of Atonement chapter. For now, suffice it to say that the qualifications for the priests were many, and one of those things that set them apart was their clothing. For example, only the priests in the temple wore pure white linen.

At the Passover meal, the father or the male head of the home leads the Seder. (Pronounced say'-der, Seder is another word often used to refer to the Passover meal. It literally means "order.") The Passover meal follows a specific order and a haggadah (which means "the telling" and is a booklet that contains the order of the meal) is usually provided for each participant. There are many types of haggadot (plural of haggadah), including lengthy, detailed ones that list many blessings and responsorial readings, ones that are short and "just the basics," some for children that have coloring pages included to keep their interest throughout the meal, and even quite a few to choose from that are Messianic in nature including all the symbolisms that point to Jesus as the Messiah. The choice of haggadah is up to the leader.

The leader of the Seder, acting somewhat as the high priest as he leads his family through the meal, wears a kittel. The kittel is a white garment symbolizing purity and forgiveness. It is also worn by the rabbis on Yom

Kippur, by a groom on his wedding day, and by some who elect to be buried in it.

Read John 13:1-5.

1. What did Jesus do before washing the disciples' feet (v. 4)?

____

____

This outer garment that Jesus removed was probably a kittel. If, indeed, Jesus was wearing a kittel at the Last Supper, He was dressed as a high priest worthy to lead the meal. He was also dressed as a bridegroom ready to receive His bride. And, He was dressed ready for death. Jesus fulfilled all of these roles for us. Interestingly, in the Bible, one other group of people is described as being dressed in fine linen.

Discover who it is in Revelation 19:7-9.

____

Later in this chapter, we'll learn about both ancient and current wedding customs of the Jewish people. It was learning about these wedding traditions that first sparked our interest in studying the feasts of Israel and enhanced our understanding of God's love for us. At that time, we began studying these feasts by looking carefully at the Feast of Passover.

The Passover meal, as with most celebratory meals, begins with the lighting of candles. It is traditional at Passover that a woman lights the candles. This has always been interesting to us, since it was a woman, Mary, who brought Jesus, the light of the world, into this world. Since it's not completely clear when this tradition started, it is hard to know if a woman lit the candles for the disciples at their last supper with Jesus. Dallas likes to believe that surely a woman prepared the meal for the men dining in her upper room and may have been asked to come up and light the candles for them. What a great cook she must have been, and what pleasure to be serving the heroes of the day! After all, Jesus had been heralded into Jerusalem to shouts of "Hosanna!" just a few days prior. Did she visit with them for a moment? Was there great joy or a sense of tension in the room? Would she still have entertained such important guests if she had known one of them would be publicly tried and crucified the next day?

In the Passover meal, there are four cups of wine (or kosher grape juice) consumed throughout the meal. The first is the cup of sanctification. This is followed by the cup of deliverance, the cup of redemption, and the cup of praise. We will consider the meaning behind each of these cups throughout this chapter as we savor the many symbolisms in this feast.

A PASSIONATE LOVE SANCTIFIES

The first cup, the **cup of sanctification**, begins the Passover meal and sets it apart as holy. Jesus is holy and is set apart as our high priest. He is not only worthy to be the sacrificial lamb, but is also, at the same time, sanctified to be the high priest offering the sacrifice.

Read Hebrews 8:1-2 and Hebrews 9:11-14.

1. How does the author of Hebrews describe Christ in Chapter 8 and in 9:11?

____

____

2. How did Christ enter the holy place (9:12)?

____

____

3. What qualified Him to enter this way (9:14)?

____

____

____

4. What does this mean for us (9:14)?

____

____

Read Hebrews 13:11-16.

5. Being sanctified as our high priest, what did Jesus do for us outside the gate?

____

6. What, then, is our responsibility (or sacrifice)?

____

In modern Israel, "outside the gate," beyond the walls of the Old City of Jerusalem, within close proximity to what many believe to be Golgotha (or the Place of the Skull) where Jesus was crucified, is a very noisy bus stop. The crowds waiting for the buses are a flurry of raucous activity, children kicking wadded up trash "balls" in a disjointed game of street soccer, babies crying, workers calling to one another over the noise and fumes of the diesel bus motors. Juxtaposed with this commotion, however, is the site of the Garden Tomb. We were fortunate, during our visit to Israel, to explore this garden and its empty tomb. Let us take you back in time and share with you the solemn, divinely appointed moments we experienced during our time there:

Surrounded by large, scenic hedges and protected from the nearby uproar of the bus stop, rests this beautiful serene garden. A tomb, believed by many to be the one where Jesus' body was laid to rest after His death, is hewn from the edge of the garden's limestone terrain. The small, white-stone room aglow in soft light coming from the little window carved in the outer wall beckons us to step inside Jesus' tomb. The quiet tranquility bids us listen closely. Is that a brush of recent angel wings just beyond our touch or a soft wrinkle of fabric smoothed into a neat fold just outside of our hearing? The boundary between our realm and God's eternity is one breath, and time inside the tomb seems as if we have just missed the Lord's presence by a breath, a heartbeat.

We are amazed to so profoundly feel the living existence of Jesus in the midst of this residence of death.

Memory of the rowdy bus stop long forgotten, we step reverently out of the tomb and wander aimlessly through the garden. It is exquisitely manicured, fragrantly blooming in abundance. Lovely, quiet alcoves intermittently appear, tucked along the meandering pathways. It is within one of these niches that true worship takes place for us. We are seated, taking a small piece of bread, drinking juice from a little olive-wood cup, remembering the death of our Jesus, and feeling the risen presence of His Spirit. Through the foliage, among the flowers from the far side of the garden we barely hear the melodic voices of other visitors. They are fellow sojourners drawn from the deafening, discordant earth, meeting the One "outside the gate" to find harmony and cool respite within the garden. We don't understand the words they sing. They are Japanese, maybe. The melody we recognize; it is worshipful, reflective, intimate. We join them in the familiar hymn, each in our native tongue, yet both in one language of love:

I come to the garden alone
While the dew is still on the roses
And the voice I hear falling on my ear
The Son of God discloses.

And He walks with me, and He talks with me,
And He tells me I am His own;
And the joy we share as we tarry there,
None other has ever known.
~ C. Austin Miles, 1912

We have walked with Him this day, felt His presence in the garden. We long to continue to meet Him outside the gate, "bearing His reproach. For here we do not have a lasting city, but we are seeking the city which is to come. Through Him then, let us continually offer up a sacrifice of praise to God … " (Hebrews 13:13-14).

Today, away from the boisterous, bus-stop part of your life, set apart some time to offer a sacrifice of thanks and praise to God. Thank Him for everything in your life that holds peace and beauty.

GARDEN TOMB

As stated above, the first cup of sanctification set the meal apart as holy. We saw Jesus sanctified as our high priest. He is holy and set apart. Following the drinking of this first cup of wine is a ritual washing of the hands. While all the participants take part in this hand washing later in the meal, this specific instance is reserved only for the host, or the leader, of the Seder. It is to show that he is the most important person at the table, and that he is worthy to lead the others in the Passover. It was probably at this place in the meal that Jesus took off His outer garment and washed the feet of His disciples. We read about that in John 13:3-5.

Read John 13:3-17.

1. What is Peter's reaction to Jesus washing his feet?

____

2. What are we supposed to learn from Jesus washing the disciples' feet (John 13:14-17)?

____

____

Peter's initial refusal to allow Jesus to wash his feet became more understandable once we realized the significance of the moment in the meal that it probably took place. At the very point in the Seder that Jesus could have exalted Himself as worthy and important by the ceremonial washing of His hands, He chose to play the part of the servant by washing the disciples' feet. Jesus chooses to serve us. He loves us. He loves us with boundless abandon, and He chose to prove it at the very moment when He could have taken all the glory for Himself!

After drinking the cup of sanctification and the ceremonial washing of hands, some various symbolic foods are eaten. A seder plate adorns the table and contains a roasted egg, the shank bone of a lamb, charoset (a deliciously sweet mixture of chopped apples, nuts, and honey), parsley, and maror (bitter herbs, usually horseradish and romaine lettuce). Each of these items has particular significance.

The roasted egg reminds the Jewish people of the destruction of the temple. We will learn more about the roasted egg and the background and timing of its appearance on the seder plate in the chapter on First Fruits. The shank bone of a lamb is also present as a reminder that when the people had a temple, they would have sacrificed a lamb. It is not coincidence that a shank bone was chosen as this reminder. The Hebrew word for this shank bone is "zeroah," meaning "arm," and is the same word used to describe the outstretched arm of God that delivered the Jews from bondage in Egypt. As believers in Christ, we see this symbolism as Yeshua (Jesus) stretching out His arms on the cross to deliver us from sin.

The parsley is dipped twice in salt water and eaten. Several explanations are common for this practice. A couple of our favorites include: 1) the parsley represents the hyssop that was dipped in the blood to put on the doorposts, and 2) the parsley is dipped in the saltwater representing the Hebrews passing through the Red Sea, and the parsley is dipped again into the saltwater symbolizing the Egyptians who tried to follow. The parsley is quickly eaten, though, as the Egyptians didn't make it safely across.

The charoset, with its chopped apples and nuts, resembles coarse brick mortar, and that's exactly what the word means — brick mortar. Charoset reminds the Jews that they had to start making their own brick mortar after Moses asked Pharaoh to let them go. It also reminds them of the bitterness of slavery. We might ask why something that tastes so good would remind them of something so bitter. One explanation is that when deliverance is imminent, even the hardest task seems possible. When we observe Passover at our house, we eat the charoset to remind us that some sin seems sweet. We don't necessarily like giving up certain sin, but it is still sin and burdens us like having to make our own brick mortar.

Maror is eaten to remember the bitterness of slavery; we remember the bitterness of sin. One food, in particular, is ground horseradish. If you've eaten ground horseradish, you know it cleans out your sinuses. Jesus and His disciples were probably at this spot in the meal when Jesus identified His betrayer.

Read John 13:21-30.

3. When did Judas leave the Passover meal?

____

There is a time during the meal that a piece of unleavened bread (matzah) is dipped in the horseradish. Our children usually warn "first-timers" at our Passover meal to watch out for the "white stuff" (the ground horseradish). They know it's hot! Probably, this matzah dipped in the horseradish is what Jesus used to identify Judas as His betrayer. Since Judas left as soon as he ate it, he fled with a taste of bitterness in his mouth. Most likely his eyes were watering, his nose was dripping, and his mouth was burning. Sin affects all of our senses. Poor Judas, if only he would have stayed in the presence of the Lord and calmed his pain with the next cup in the Passover meal.

CHAPTER THREE

PASSOVER, PART 2
(Pesach)

— *A Lesson on Eternal Love*

In the previous chapter, we saw Jesus play the part of the high priest as well as the Passover Lamb suffering outside the gate. We also briefly touched on the four cups of wine taken throughout the meal: 1) sanctification, 2) deliverance, 3) redemption, and 4) praise. These cups and this Passover meal have so much meaning for observant Jews. As Christians, we remember these things were set up as a copy and shadow of heavenly things, but the substance is Christ, our Savior.

ETERNAL LOVE IS ENOUGH

The **cup of deliverance**, the second cup, reminded the Israelites that they had been delivered from the bondage of slavery. The wine at the Passover is red and is served at room temperature. It is a perfect symbol of blood. Each cup is filled to the top, as a full cup of wine is a symbol of joy in Jewish culture. However, this second cup is first spilled out on a white plate a little at a time with the reading of each plague, symbolizing the sorrow of both

Egyptians and Israelites as the 10 plagues of blood, frogs, lice, flies, pestilence, boils, hail, locusts, darkness, and the death of the first born were poured out on the people. Nevertheless, the Israelites were delivered from Egypt, so this second cup is refilled to the top before drinking it to remember with great joy their deliverance from slavery.

What a clear picture this is of what Jesus did for us! The white plate, symbolizing purity by its white color, is covered with the wine, a symbol of blood, as it is poured out. The perfect, pure, spotless Lamb of God spilled His blood for us to save us from all kinds of sorrows that plague our lives. He suffered so that we may have joy. We have deliverance from the bondage of sin through the spilled blood of Jesus, our Passover Lamb.

One of the traditional songs sung at Passover is "Dayenu" (pronounced die-a-new). The word means "It is enough" or "It would have been sufficient." There are many verses sung recalling the deliverance from each plague and finally the freedom from Egypt. The verses continue recounting the crossing of the Red Sea and even the provision of manna in the desert. All the while, the chorus chants, "Dayenu." It is enough. The idea is that it would have been sufficient if God had provided deliverance from only one plague, or even two. It would have been enough if God had provided relief from slavery or escape from the Egyptians. But God didn't stop there. He continued to provide other gifts of divine mercy: manna in the desert, shelter, water, victory over foes, just like He continues to provide all things in overwhelming abundance for us. However, if our health isn't perfect, or our family is falling apart, or loved ones are sick or dying, we would do well to have the mindset of the Israelites, being satisfied that deliverance from death is enough. God provided us a Messiah, a deliverer from eternal death. Jesus is our Dayenu, and His grace is sufficient (2 Corinthians 12:9-10). Jesus is enough!

Read through 1 Peter 1:3-25.

1. From these verses, list things you are thankful for, ways God has provided for you, and thoughts that remind you, "Jesus is enough."
I am thankful for:

____

____

God has provided:

____

____

____

Jesus is enough!

____

Another traditional part of Passover is the asking of four questions. The youngest child who can read typically reads the questions aloud. This eventually gives each child in the family a turn at participating in this honor. The four questions are then answered by the father or the leader of the meal. These questions present the opportunity for recounting the history of the Passover in the telling of the answers. The four questions and their answers follow.

1) Q: Why is this night different than any other night? Why on this night do we eat only unleavened bread? A: The salvation from Egypt came so quickly that there was no time for the dough to rise.

As Christians, we now wait expectantly for the triumphant return of Christ, and we need to be diligent to purge the leaven (sin) from our lives.

2) Q: On any other night we eat any kind of herb. Why tonight do we eat only bitter herbs? A: We eat bitter herbs to remind us of the bitterness of slavery in Egypt.

As Christians, we remember the bitterness of sin and death from which the Messiah freed us.

3) Q: On all other nights, we do not dip our vegetable even once. Why tonight do we dip them twice? A: We dip the parsley twice in the salt water to remember the tears shed in bondage in Egypt.

As Christians, we remember that the Messiah turned tears of sadness into expressions of joy for our lives.

4) Q: On all other nights we eat sitting up. Why tonight do we eat reclining? A: We recline because in ancient times it was the posture of free people. Those liberated in the exodus from Egypt were no longer slaves.

As Christians, we are free from the penalty of sin, which is death. We have rest in the Messiah!

We read Hebrews 4:1-16 in the chapter on Sabbath, noting the theme of "rest" in these passages. Return to those verses and consider the following questions.

2. What keeps people from entering God's rest (vv. 1-6)?

___

___

3. What privileges have we been given if we believe in Jesus as our high priest (v. 16)?

___

___

Have you entered God's rest? He has provided for you in abundance. He has passionately shown His love for you with boundless abandon. Draw near to Him and enjoy His grace and His rest today. Dayenu. He is enough!

ETERNAL LOVE TAKES A BRIDE

Following the drinking of the first two cups of wine and partaking in the symbolic foods, a great meal is served, a wonderful buffet of traditional foods. We've considered the first two cups of Passover. In this section, let's look at the third cup of Passover. The **cup of redemption** is typically thought to be the one that Christians choose to pull out of Passover as the parallel to our communion cup. The Israelites were redeemed from their old life of slavery in Egypt. We are redeemed from our old life of sin that leads to death, and we are given new life.

In the Old Testament, covenants (or contracts) made with God involved the shedding of blood. You can read about the covenant God made with

Abraham in Genesis 15 and 17, and the covenant with Moses and Aaron in Exodus 24. It's fitting that at the Last Supper, a Passover meal, Jesus chose both a cup of wine and the imagery of blood to create a new covenant with us. Luke 22:20 says, "And in the same way He took the cup after they had eaten, saying, 'This cup which is poured out for you is the new covenant in My blood.'"

Read Hebrews 8:10-13.

1. What is Jesus' new covenant (vv. 10-13)?

____

____

____

God will indeed write His law upon our hearts. It is with our heart that we choose to passionately seek Jesus. Interestingly, a certain circumstance that involves a cup of wine and a contract is a part of Jewish wedding customs. Remember, Jesus was dressed to be a bridegroom if He had on a kittel at Passover. If Jesus would have come as an American in the 21st century, maybe He would have used wedding imagery that included a diamond solitaire ring for a proposal with His audiences, but He came as a Jewish man and He used experiences with which a Jewish listener would be familiar. The Bible refers to believers as the bride of Christ on several occasions. Wouldn't it be interesting to envision exactly what that meant in Jesus' mind in a Jewish culture! Let's take a look at some of these wedding traditions of the Jewish people and see what we can learn from them and how they relate to the Passover meal and to us today.

Jews have been marrying strangers for thousands of years. Read the story of Rebekah and Isaac in Genesis 24:1-67.

2. Did Rebekah know Isaac? ______ Had she ever seen him? ______

On what do you think she based her decision to go to a faraway land to marry a stranger?

____

____

1. What gifts did Abraham send with his servant (vv. 10, 22, 53)?

____

____

2. What did Rebekah do when she saw Isaac (v. 65)?

____

____

Rebekah married a stranger, Isaac. Abraham wanted a bride for his son from his own people. He sent his servant 500 miles to find a bride. When Rebekah saw the gifts from Isaac, she agreed to go on a long journey to a place she had never been to marry someone she had never met. Believers in Jesus have made a similar commitment. We have agreed to go to a faraway place (Heaven) to be the bride of someone we have never met face to face (Jesus). While we have not actually seen the Bridegroom, we have seen His gifts. We have the greatest gift: the Holy Spirit. We also have the fruits of the Spirit: love, joy, peace, patience, kindness, goodness, faithfulness, gentleness, and self-control (Galatians 5:22-23). If that's not enough, we have read accounts of eyewitnesses relating the great works and signs that Jesus miraculously performed while He walked on this earth. In fact, Jesus Himself said, "Believe Me that I am in the Father, and the Father in Me; otherwise believe on account of the works themselves" (John 14:11).

Another great wedding story in the Old Testament is that of Jacob and Rachel. Just like Jacob's father Isaac who received his bride from relatives in a distant land, so, too, Jacob finds his bride among relatives in the land of Haran. However, she is also a stranger to Jacob, just as Rebekah had been a stranger to Isaac.

Read this story in Genesis 29:1-30.

3. What price did Jacob agree to pay for Rachel (v. 20)?

____

4. What did Laban do in honor of the wedding (v. 22)?

____

5. Who did Jacob actually wake up with the next morning (v. 25)?

____

6. What did Laban further require of Jacob to acquire Rachel (v. 27)?

____

7. What was the total price Jacob paid for Rachel (v. 30)?

____

This story is the first recorded occurrence of a wedding party. It also sets the stage for traditional wedding customs in Judaism for centuries to come: marry within the clan, celebrate with a week-long feast, one might pay a high price for the one he loves, and the wedding vows still count even if there is no love. (In traditional Judaism, the woman had no legal authority to divorce her husband.) Jesus has called us to be His bride. He paid a high price for us, and there's nothing that can separate us from His love (Romans 8:38-39).

Documentation at least as far back as Talmudic times (100-400 A.D.), proves that blessings over a cup of wine and the signing of a contract was a part of the wedding ceremony. A blessing over a cup of wine began the betrothal period, which was legally binding and usually lasted one year. If a young man wanted to marry a girl, he might follow her home and pour her a cup of wine. Just as we would understand a diamond ring offered as a proposal, so the young woman would recognize this cup as a proposal. If she drank the wine, she agreed to marry him. A contract (ketubah) was also signed at this time, and money changed hands. Then the bride began to wear a veil to let others know she was spoken for. Another cup of wine would be blessed and shared at the actual ceremony.

The money paid for a bride was a high price, maybe equivalent to what we might think of as a down payment for a house. The groom may consult his own father concerning this payment, seeking his judgment on the settlement of a fair price. After all, it is a weighty commitment. We see Jesus playing this role, consulting His Father to discuss the price for His bride. In Matthew 26:39 Jesus says, "… My Father, if it is possible, let this cup pass from Me; yet not as I will, but as Thou wilt." If Jesus would have come as an American, He may have said, "Let this *ring* pass from me." The cup of deliverance from the Passover meal that Jesus said was going to be poured out for us as a new covenant can also symbolize the cup of wine offered to the bride as a proposal. The price connected to the offer was Jesus' life — a high price indeed, worthy of consulting His Father.

Wine, a contract, and a separation period are still a part of the wedding traditions today, although only a week of separation is required. During this period, the bride and groom cannot see each other. On the wedding day, the groom signs a ketubah, then sees his bride for the first time in a week. At this time, he draws the veil over her face while friends and family look on and a rabbi recites a blessing. After this, the bride stays veiled throughout the ceremony. There are several origins attributed to this custom of veiling the bride. One is that the groom should be sure whom he is marrying and not be fooled as Jacob was with Leah; another is that Rebekah veiled herself upon seeing Isaac.

We have been bought with a high price, the blood of Jesus. First Corinthians 6:17-20 reminds us, "But the one who joins himself to the Lord is one spirit with Him .... For you have been bought with a price: therefore glorify God in your body." We are spoken for, and we should look the part by "wearing a veil."

Read Colossians 3:12-17.

10. Record what our "veil" should look like to let others know we have been bought with a price.

____

____

After the bride has agreed to marry the groom, he tells her that he will prepare a place for her and proceeds to begin building onto his father's home a bridal chamber for his bride. He works on this under the supervision of his father, and the father is the judge of when the room is finished. What wisdom! If it were up to the groom, he would probably throw up a shack and go running back for his girl. Once again, we see Jesus acting on these very traditions. In John 13-14, when asked by Peter why he couldn't follow Jesus "right now," Jesus replies, "... In My Father's house are many dwelling places; if it were not so, I would have told you; for I go to prepare a place for you." And, concerning the coming of the Son of Man in Matthew 24:36, Jesus says, "But of that day and hour no one knows, not even the angels of heaven, nor the Son, but the Father alone.

Jesus paid the price of His life for His bride. He is with the Father preparing a place for us now. The Bridegroom has lived among us, experienced our pain, and observed our broken world firsthand. We truly believe if it were up to Jesus, He would throw up a shack and come running back for His girl, us, His bride. But, the wisdom of the Father waits for the fullness of the Gentiles to come into the inheritance of eternal life (Romans 11:25.)

While the groom is preparing a place for the bride, she begins to get her wedding party together, friends and loved ones. It is the right of the groom to return for his bride whenever his father allows, since the price has been paid. How romantic it might be to return for her at midnight! To give the bride a moment or two to get herself ready in the middle of the night, tradition dictates a shout from the groom and his friends as they near the bride's home. Knowing these traditions, several of which are still practiced today, consider the following parable.

Read Matthew 25:1-13 and 1 Thessalonians 5:2.

11. Why did the virgins become drowsy and sleep?

____

____

12. How and when will the groom come?

____

____

The foolish virgins believed the bridegroom would come; they just didn't expect him to come so soon. As a result, their oil lamps were not ready. Many theologians believe oil and the anointing of oil to be a symbol of the Holy Spirit throughout the Bible (i.e., Exodus 40:9-15, 1 John 2:20.) Many people today have heard the good news of Jesus, but not acting on this knowledge, have declined to ask for forgiveness to receive the gift of the Holy Spirit. They may believe Jesus is returning, but that they have plenty of time to make a life-changing decision, allowing Him to change their lives. Let's not make the same mistake — toying with procrastination — that the foolish virgins made. Instead, let's proclaim the name of the Bridegroom as our Lord and Savior, receiving forgiveness and the anointing of the Holy Spirit, so that we may be welcomed into the wedding feast, for we "... do not know the day nor the hour" that the Bridegroom may return for us with a shout.

In ancient times, as well as now, once the Jewish wedding ceremony is completed, some time is given for the bride and groom to be alone. The friend of the bridegroom, or the best man, guards the door for the couple, ensuring their privacy. Upon hearing the bridegroom's voice, the best man announces to the wedding attendees that "the groom's joy has been made complete." Believe it or not, our Bridegroom, Jesus, also had a best man! His name was John the Baptist.

Read John the Baptist's explanation of the Messiah in John 3:28-29 with John 17:13, 21-26.

13. What does Jesus pray for His disciples (17:13)?

____

____

14. What does Jesus pray for future believers (17:21-26)?

____

____

Finally, the bridegroom brings his wife home where they live together as husband and wife. What kind of place has our Bridegroom prepared for us?

Read Revelation 21:9-27.

15. What is the angel showing John in verse 9?

____

16. John describes the beautiful, holy city of Jerusalem. Who is its light (v. 22)?

____

17. Who walks in its light (vv. 24, 27)?

____

What an incredible mansion the Lord has prepared for us, playing the part of the Bridegroom to the very end of time! (And isn't it a fun detail that even His earthly father, Joseph, was a carpenter by trade?) At the Passover meal, Jesus sealed a new covenant with a glass of wine, the third cup of Passover, which is the cup of redemption. It is this cup of redemption that Jesus blessed at the Passover meal He shared with His disciples and proclaimed to be His "blood of the covenant, which is poured out for many for the forgiveness of sin" (Matthew 26:28).

Christ indeed redeemed us through His blood by being crucified on the cross, thus beginning a new covenant with us. The next time you take communion, picture Jesus standing before you, sliding a proposal cup of wine over to you. "Will you be my Bride?" He asks. "Will you wear a veil to show that you have been bought with a price? Will you be ready for me when I return for you with a shout like a thief in the night?" You are the Bride of Christ. He so passionately loves you and longs for your name to be written in the Lamb's book of life.

Read Ephesians 5:25-27.

18. How did Christ love the Church?

____

19. Why did Jesus give Himself up for the church (v. 26)?

____

20. How would the church then be found?

____

Read Hebrews 9:18-28 and Hebrews 10:19-25.

21. What was present in order for both the old and new covenants to be inaugurated?

____

22. Since we have been redeemed by the blood of Christ and "have a great priest over the house of God," what should our response be (in your own words)? (Heb.10:22-25)

____

____

____

23. How has God been faithful to you?

____

____

____

24. Out of God's eternal love for you, what can you do to encourage someone today?

____

____

____

____

We have one cup of Passover yet to learn about, and we will discover more regarding it in the next section. At this point, there is another very important element that is crucial concerning Passover. That element is unleavened bread or matzah.

Leaven represents sin in the Bible. During the Passover feast and the seven days that follow, God commanded the Israelites to eat only unleavened bread. At a specific point in the Passover meal, three loaves of unleavened bread, called matzot (plural of matzah), are put into a bag that has three compartments. This bag is called a matzah tash or unity. The middle matzah is taken out, held up, and a blessing is recited over it. Then, this middle matzah is broken. Half of it is wrapped in a cloth bag and hidden away until later in the meal, at which time, typically the children hunt for it, then hold it for ransom. The meal cannot progress without it. After the host pays the ransom for this last piece of matzah, it is broken and shared with all as the dessert bread. This last piece is called the afikomen.

HAGGADAH AND MATZAH TASH WITH THREE UNLEAVENED LOAVES

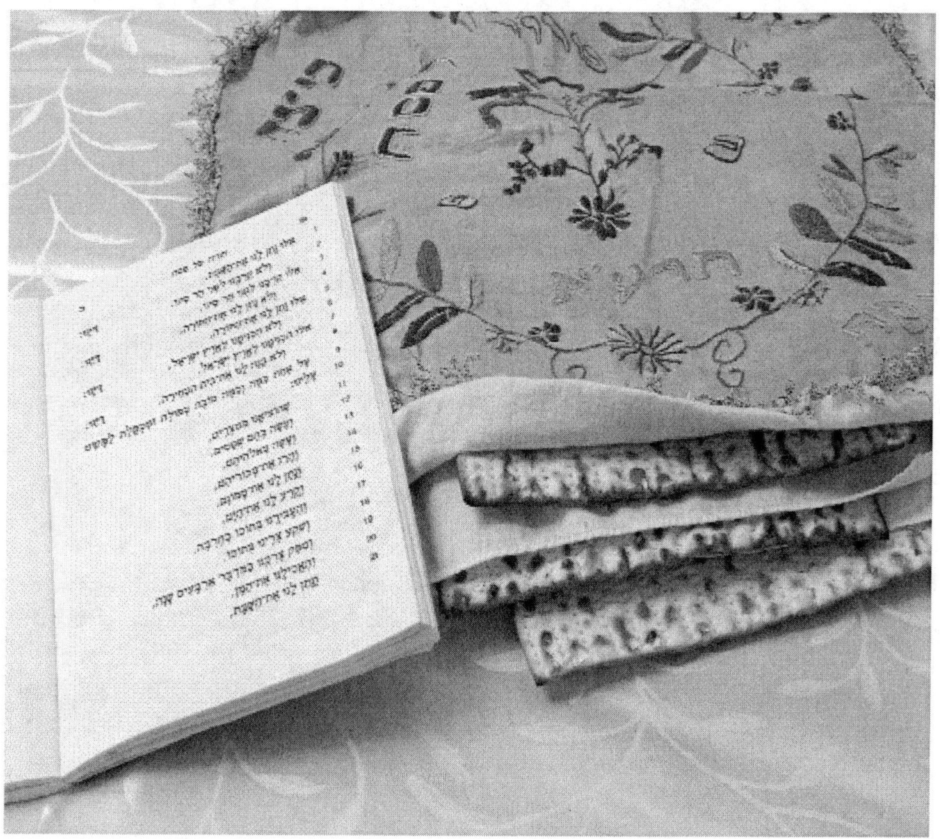

Jewish believers in Jesus as the Messiah clearly find the symbolism of the Trinity in this ceremony. The three unleavened loaves of matzah represent the Father, the Son, and the Holy Spirit. All are unleavened; all without sin. The middle matzah is a picture of Jesus. He is the only one of the Trinity that the world has literally seen. He was lifted up on a cross and His body broken. He was wrapped in linen and hidden away in a grave, but brought back from the dead on the third day. He was our ransom. Mark 10:45 tells us, "For even the Son of Man did not come to be served, but to serve, and to give His life a ransom for many." Even the word "afikomen" is significant. It means, "I have come."

In Matthew 26:26, it says, "… Jesus took some bread, and after a blessing, He broke it and gave it to the disciples, and said, 'Take, eat; this is My body.'" Here Jesus makes a great statement: "I am the afikomen. I am the middle Matzah. I am about to be broken and buried for you." The blessing that Jesus said over the bread is not recorded in the Bible. Since Jewish people had been reciting this blessing every year at Passover, there was no need to record it here. The blessing is, "Blessed are You, O Lord our God, King of the Universe, who brings forth bread from the earth." This blessing contains a great prophecy. God is in the business of bringing forth bread from the earth. Jesus called Himself the Bread of Life (John 6:35). He was even born in Bethlehem which literally means "house of bread." And, indeed, God brings forth Jesus from the earthly tomb! Jesus is our Redeemer! "Through Him, then, let us continually offer up a sacrifice of praise to God, that is, the fruit of lips that give thanks to His name" (Hebrews 13:15).

ETERNAL LOVE DESIRES OUR PRAISE

One cup of wine remains for all to drink and complete the Passover feast. It is the **cup of praise**. However, a lone goblet waits patiently at a prominent place setting. It has gone untouched throughout the meal. It is the Cup of Elijah. Jewish people believe that the prophet Elijah will return before the Messiah comes, and it would be a great time for him to come during the Seder. In case he comes, they set a place for him at the Passover table. To be sure they haven't missed him, the children are sent to look for him, opening the front door to make sure he's not waiting there.

When our children were little, we celebrated Passover with some other families with young children. When the children had hunted for the afikomen earlier in the Seder, one of them found it and was handsomely rewarded as Carl paid the money for the ransom so the meal could continue. Now, with great gusto the children raced to the front door, this time to look for Elijah. They ran out into the yard looking fervently for him. We hustled them back inside, and Dallas overheard one of them ask another, "Who found him? Where was he?" They were understandably confused, just as the disciples were when they asked Jesus about Elijah.

This belief that Elijah will return before the coming Messiah is based on the scripture found in Malachi 4:5, "Behold, I am going to send you Elijah the prophet before the coming of the great and terrible day of the Lord." Read how Jesus addressed this concern among the Jews of His day in the following verses.

Read Matthew 11:7-14, Mark 9:13, and Luke 1:13-17.

1. Who does Jesus say came in the "spirit and power of Elijah"?

____

With the search for Elijah over, the Seder is almost ended. As we discussed at the beginning of this chapter, God's initial covenant with Abraham was signed with the blood of animals, as was the covenant with Moses. The new covenant introduced at the Last Supper was signed with the blood of Jesus.

Read Matthew 26:29-30.

In these verses, Jesus says He "will not drink of this fruit of the vine from now on until that day when I drink it new with you in My Father's kingdom." He needed to explain why He wasn't drinking the last cup of Passover. He had to spill His blood and fulfill the cup of redemption before drinking the fourth and last cup of Passover. The last cup of Passover is the cup of praise. It is also sometimes called "the cup of ushering in the new kingdom." Isn't it encouraging that Jesus says He will drink it new with us in His Father's kingdom! The Jewish people raise this cup with the toast, "Next year in Jerusalem!" They are hoping for an opportunity to observe this feast in Jerusalem as it was meant to be celebrated. We can hope for a soon return of the Lamb to the new Jerusalem where we can praise Him and usher in His new kingdom.

2. From Matthew 26:29-30, what was the last thing Jesus and the disciples did before going out to the Mount of Olives?

____

Until we learned about Passover, we wondered what hymn the disciples may have sung with Jesus. Now we know that the traditional Passover meal closes with the singing of the Hallel, "Praise Thou the Lord," which is from Psalms 113 through 118. Keep in mind that this probably was the hymn the Lord and His disciples were singing as they went out to the Mount of Olives.

Read through and meditate on Psalms 113 through 118.

3. Write down some of the verses that might have comforted Christ specifically, since He knew His death was near at hand. Also, take note of phrases that point directly to Jesus or prophesy of Him specifically.

____

____

____

____

One of our favorite passages from the Hallel is one that came to have new meaning for us when we realized the context and history of these psalms. Psalms 118:24 says, "This is the day which the Lord has made; let us rejoice and be glad in it." We grew up singing this as a praise song in church. We interpreted it to mean that we should be thankful for every day we've been given and to rejoice in each day. While this is certainly true, thinking of Jesus possibly singing this song on the very day that He was headed to change the old covenant of law to a new covenant of grace definitely makes us rejoice in *that* day. What a glorious celebration to drink the last cup of Passover with the risen Lord as we usher in the new kingdom!

"Next year in Jerusalem!"

CHAPTER FOUR

UNLEAVENED BREAD (Matzah)

— *A Lesson on Sin*

Licking and sticking and shopping for toys. Dallas remembers spending time at her grandma's house playing for hours outside in the garden, but she also spent time at the kitchen table licking green stamps, or running them atop a damp yellow sponge and sticking them in little booklets. What's interesting is that Dallas' daddy owned a grocery store, and she also remembers that just days before sticking these very stamps in a book at her grandma's, she had dialed them out of the little box at the grocery store where her grandma had been a customer. Back then, grocery stores gave out green stamps according to how much you spent in their store. You could take the stamps, stick them in a little book that was also provided, and then redeem them at a green stamp store.

The green stamp store had all kinds of things: dishes, toasters, blenders, camping and picnic supplies, but most importantly, it had toys! The green stamp store also had a catalog you could browse through at home. It was wishing for those treasures in the catalog that kept you licking and sticking those yucky tasting stamps. The green stamp store didn't take cash or credit cards; you could only trade in your stamps for what you wanted. It was a great lesson in redemption. The stamps were worthless if you held on to them. You couldn't use them anywhere else at any other store. But, if you put them in a book and redeemed them, you received whatever the store had to offer.

The lesson of redemption is taught many times in many ways throughout the Bible. One of the most prominent is that Jesus redeems us from sin. If we give up our sin through confession and repentance, He gives us all the mercies and grace His kingdom has to offer. And we don't have to lick any yucky tasting stamps — all we have to do is receive it.

REMOVING SIN

In the previous chapter, we discovered how Jesus fulfilled Passover by being the perfect Lamb of God, and that because of His blood, the angel of death will "pass over" those who belong to Him. As we complete this chapter, take into consideration how Jesus completes this second Jewish feast of Unleavened Bread.

Read Leviticus 23: 4-8.

1. When does the Feast of Unleavened Bread begin, and how long does it last?

   ____

2. What were they commanded to do on this festival?

   ____

The feast of Unleavened Bread is the second feast listed by God in Leviticus 23. The feasts of Passover and Unleavened Bread are very closely associated. They are so much a part of each other that their names are used interchangeably to refer to the entire eight-day festival period. Unleavened Bread begins the day after Passover, on the 15th of

Nissan. Following the commandments, the Hebrews ate only unleavened bread for the seven days of this festival.

Read Exodus 12:15-20.

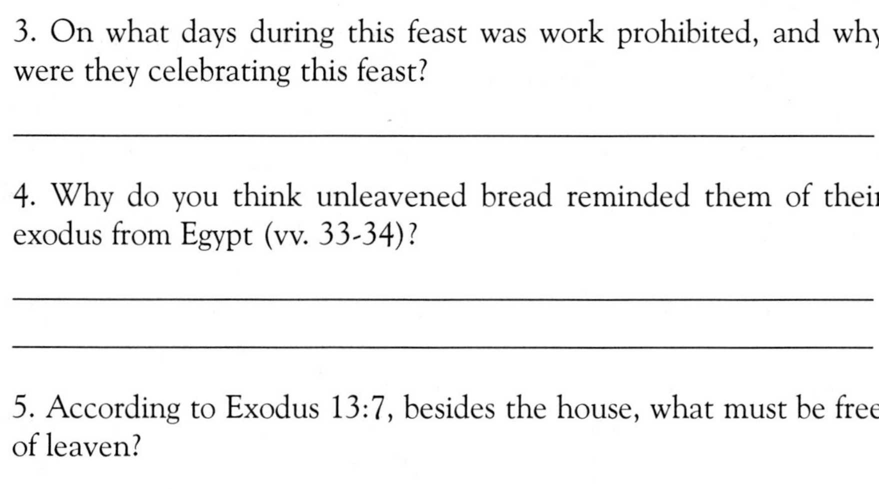

3. On what days during this feast was work prohibited, and why were they celebrating this feast?

4. Why do you think unleavened bread reminded them of their exodus from Egypt (vv. 33-34)?

5. According to Exodus 13:7, besides the house, what must be free of leaven?

The Hebrew people who left Egypt had been slaves, and their heritage for the past 400 years was one of slavery. It's doubtful that the Egyptians spent much money or time educating the Hebrews. Reminding these people of their history would have been an inherent problem. God designed these annual feasts for the people to have a hands-on history lesson reminding them of His great deliverance. Because they left Egypt in such haste, there was not time for their bread to rise. At this time every year for thousands of years, they would eat unleavened bread after observing Passover to remember this detail. What a great master-teacher God is!

In the previous chapter, we discussed the preparation needed before Passover began. One very important detail we did not discuss is purging the house of all leaven. The Jewish people are forbidden to have any leaven in their homes (Exodus 12:19) or in their possession (Ex.13:7) during this feast. So, a thorough housecleaning is in order. This is not a "quick run-through" cleaning. This deep cleaning is probably where we get the concept of spring cleaning. In fact, some ultra-orthodox communities go so far as to re-paint the insides of their homes.

Ridding the Jewish home of leaven isn't enough. During Passover, you must remember to clean your car, your office, even your briefcase. And how about your pets? Yes, also the food for household pets or livestock must be leaven-free! It is not that the animals are restricted from eating leaven, but that people cannot benefit from the use of leaven during this week if it means using leavened, ready-made food for their pets. Small pieces of leaven could even be trapped in your toothbrush, so new toothbrushes are sometimes a part of this week's celebration as well.

Leaven includes yeast, but also any product made with any of the five major grains (wheat, rye, barley, oats, and spelt). Anything made from these grains is considered leavened. Any grain or flour that has been in contact with water for more than 18 minutes has started the leavening process. You can buy special matzah made for Passover to ensure that no more than 18 minutes has elapsed between mixing dry ingredients with water and cooking.

By noon on the 14th of Nissan, all leaven must be removed. Can you imagine running a business that requires you to own a large amount of leaven? Perhaps you might own a bakery. What would you do with all the leavened products you are going to need back in one week? You may need to take advantage of a modern procedure creating the option for "selling" leaven to a friendly gentile (Goy). In fact, you can easily find Rabbi-approved leaven contracts online. In this way, you still possess the leaven, but it is not "technically" yours. Then, you can buy it back at the end of the week.

Isn't this a vivid picture of what we sometimes try to do with our sin? We blame others for it by denying our ownership of it. We ask forgiveness for it and give it over to God, only to take it back again at the end of the day or week. It seems to be fairly easy to give up the big sins — most of us aren't serial killers. But the small crumbs of sin that cling to the bottoms of our pockets and stick to our toothbrush, like the money we are selfish with and the hateful words that come from our mouths, we must give to the Lord — without a contract for buying them back.

Many Jewish people remember Passover and Unleavened Bread for its housecleaning and dishwashing more than anything else. This act of removing all of the leaven from their homes outwardly demonstrates the purging of sin from their lives.

For Dallas, cleaning the house becomes overwhelming if she lets it get too messy with too many chores to tackle. Sometimes there is so much to do she doesn't know where to start, so she simply doesn't do anything. It's paralyzing. She does neither what she should nor what she wants. Isn't sin similar? When we refuse to deal with it, leaving it to clutter our thinking and to make many areas of our lives messy, it becomes overwhelming. Sin paralyzes us from serving others, from worshipping unhindered, from praying intimately, from being obedient. We begin to do neither what we ought nor what we want. Confessing sin quickly and repenting of it cleanses our heart's home, allowing us to both serve and relax in an uncluttered, beautiful space.

Once the house is clean, the leaven-purging becomes a game for the children. Cookie or bread crumbs are placed around the house, and the kids search for them. When they find some, their father uses a feather to sweep the leaven into a wooden spoon. Then he wraps the spoon and crumbs in linen and burns it in a fire. This burning of leaven acts out the judgment of sin.

Several different traditions are associated with this act of searching for leaven. We like the particular custom of searching in the dark for the leaven while using only a candle for light. It's not evident that the leaven is anywhere in the home until the light shines upon it. Isn't that just like the sin in our own heart's home? We aren't even aware of some sins in our lives until the light of Christ shines upon it, making it very evident to us. After finding and burning the leaven, the father makes the following nullification statement: "All leaven that is in my possession that I did not see and did not destroy, let it be null and ownerless as the dust of the earth." What amazing symbolism and application to our own lives: As followers of Christ, when God's radiance reveals our sin, we need to be sure to turn it quickly over to Him, asking forgiveness and relinquishing ownership of it. When we do that, sin can no longer exercise its power over us, just as the Jewish father's prayer makes the power of any hidden, remaining leaven null.

Why is God so concerned about leaven anyway? Leaven is simply yeast or a rising agent used in cooking. Why does He want it out of the lives of the Israelites for one week? To answer these questions, it is important to understand how the Bible speaks about leaven symbolically.

Read Leviticus 2:11.

6. What was God's law regarding leaven and the grain offerings?

____

Read Matthew 16:1-12 and Mark 8:15.

7. When Jesus spoke of leaven, what did the disciples think he was talking about?

____

8. Jesus warned His disciples to beware of the leaven of whom?

a.________________ b. __________________ c. ________________

9. In Luke 12:1-2, Jesus defines the leaven of the Pharisees as that of hypocrisy. Using Mark 6:14-29, Mark 12:18, and Acts 23:6-8, do you have any possible answers that might identify the leaven of the other two groups?

a. Pharisees: *hypocrisy*
b. Herod: __________________
c. Sadducees: _______________

The major use of leaven in the Bible is as a symbol for sin. While many different types of sin exist, all their effects are similar. If we allow a seed of unbelief to creep into our thinking, or a motive of desiring the praise of others to direct our actions, we quickly find ourselves in a messy, cluttered space of disobedience and separation from an intimate relationship with the Lord.

Read 1 Corinthians 5:6-8.

10. What can we learn about how leaven works in this verse?

____

____

11. Using this information, how does sin act in our lives?

____

____

____

12. In these verses, Paul calls us "unleavened." What gives us the right to that title?

____

____

13. What does it mean to "celebrate the feast"?

____

Passover is Jesus. We celebrate Passover by accepting Him as our sacrifice "once for all" (Romans 6:10-11). We celebrate Unleavened Bread by putting away leaven. Getting even the "small" sin out of our lives is important since it permeates every aspect of our lives and sours us if we hang onto it. Because Jesus took away our sins and made us "unleavened," we can now live with sincerity and truthfulness.

We don't have to live like the Pharisees, believing in the supernatural and a resurrection, yet hypocritical in the way we live our lives. Nor should we be like the Sadducees who were sinful in their unbelief, or like Herod who was worldly and unrepentant even though he liked John and the words that he spoke. We are forgiven. Now that's something to celebrate!

To understand how Jesus fulfills the feasts of Unleavened Bread, consider what was happening to Jesus during this feast.

Read Matthew 27:45-66.

14. Jesus was crucified on Passover. Remembering that the Jewish day begins at evening, what day was beginning as Joseph of Arimathea laid Jesus in the tomb?

____

15. From today's study, what insight do you have as to how Jesus fulfills the feast of Unleavened Bread?

____

____

Read Isaiah 53:5-6.

Jesus redeemed us by His blood, and His blood was shed in more ways than one. Specific details of some of those ways were prophesied in Isaiah 53. Complete the following information from these verses.

For our transgressions He was______________________,
For our iniquities (sin) He was ____________________,
For our healing He was __________________________,
All our iniquity has fallen on ______________________.

Remember from the Passover lesson, Jesus referred to Himself as matzah: the middle, unleavened bread from the matzah tash. This unleavened bread is a great picture of Jesus and a detailed illustration of these verses in Isaiah. Matzah is unleavened, sinless. It is pierced in the cooking process. It has brown blotches on it as if it is bruised. It is striped and finally crushed so that it can be shared with all. Sinless, pierced, striped, bruised, crushed: Jesus. He is the Bread of Life!

On Passover, Jesus was pierced, scourged, bruised and crushed. Death by crucifixion usually took several days and was a slow, agonizing death. However, severely injured and weakened by the beatings from His captors, Jesus died in only six hours. He had a feast to keep. When He was hanging on the cross, he took on our sins. Having become sin for us, Jesus had to be in the tomb before sundown because that is when the Feast of Unleavened Bread began. Just as leaven was wrapped in linen and hidden away, so too, Jesus was wrapped in linen and hidden away in a tomb before the beginning of the Feast of Unleavened Bread. Even in the midst of sin and suffering, God controlled every circumstance surrounding Jesus' crucifixion, including the timing of His death, using it to fulfill a feast set up many generations before.

When we focus on our own sin and pain, it is easy to forget that the God of the Universe is still in control. Allowing God to take our sin and hide it away frees us to concentrate, not on ourselves, but on accomplishing His will for our lives and the impact we can have on others.

16. What "leaven" needs to be hidden away from your heart's home, so that God's will can be accomplished in your life?

____

RECEIVING GRACE

In the summer of 2007, Dallas' sister's house flooded. Her sister, Beverly, describes the situation this way:

> We had several days of torrential rains in our area. At the time, we were living in an older lakefront home, and we began to suspect that we might experience some flooding. Finally, one afternoon, we began to move things out of our home and take them to safer ground. Friends came with pickups and trucks, and we loaded up our most valuable things. Around two in the morning, the fire department came through the neighborhood and told us we had to leave because the water was beginning to rise and cut off access to the neighborhood. We left, feeling like we had done all we could do. Now, we could only wait.

Five days later, the rains ended and the floodwaters began to recede. I've experienced a couple of other disasters before this — a house fire and a tornado. In both of those situations, the cleanup could begin right away. But with this flood, we had to wait several days to begin the cleanup. It was very frustrating.

I will always remember the stench. The floodwaters left a layer of mud everywhere — all across the lawn and all through the house. There had been about twenty inches of water in the house, so everything from the floor up to four feet above the floor had to be removed. We decided to do the demolition ourselves in order to save the cost of a cleaning and restoration service. We scraped up tile, pulled up beautiful wood floors we had installed only six months earlier, took out carpet and all the lower cabinets in the house, along with the lower four feet of sheetrock and insulation. We also had to remove all the household items still left in the house — clothes, dishes, etc. This was in July, and it was hot and humid, and we had no air conditioning. I don't believe I have ever worked so hard in my life. We worked every day for four or five weeks from morning to night and fell asleep totally exhausted every night. There were several mornings I woke up in mid-anxiety attack.

During the first week of the demolition, there was a light rain falling almost every day, and it was so hot. We went over early one morning that week so we could get as much done as possible before it got hot. The sun had not come up yet, and I had been packing dishes and hauling them out to our SUV to take to storage. I was already hot and so tired. I was wondering if we'd really be able to do this ourselves and how long it would take. On the next trip out to the car, the sun was coming up, and even though there was a light mist, the sun was shining through the trees across the street. I stopped dead in my

> tracks, holding the box in my arms, staring at the scene. The air was literally sparkling, and the light was so beautiful. There was total silence, and it seemed like time stopped. I broke out in a huge smile, and my first thought was "My *grace is sufficient for you.*" Then tears started streaming down my cheeks. I stood for at least a couple of minutes, just watching the beautiful, sparkling light and sensing the powerful presence of God. I felt like grace was showering down on me, and I could feel my strength renewed. I'll never forget it.
>
> That was the first time in my life I began to understand what St. Therese meant when she said "everything is grace" (Therese of Lisieux, 1996). God turned what was a devastating catastrophe for our family into one of the best things that ever happened to us. What I learned in the aftermath of the flood about the sufficiency of God's grace proved to be preparation for the next difficulty we faced - my cancer diagnosis. In fact, when the doctor told me I had pancreatic cancer, I was in shock. But a thought came to me after a moment — "My *grace is sufficient for you.*" God has poured grace upon grace on me and my family. He has brought so much good out of bad. "My *grace is sufficient for you*" has brought me through countless heartbreaking moments and exhausting days. It's a thought that comes to me often, unbidden and quietly — "My *grace is sufficient for you.*" Amen.

In this section, we will find out there is always sufficient grace to take the place of the leaven in our lives. In the last section, we learned that leaven is usually a symbol for sin when used in the Bible (an example of a possible exception is Matthew 13:33). Celebrating the Feast of Unleavened Bread required removing all leaven from one's possession. Let's take a look at how King Hezekiah celebrated this feast. King Hezekiah came to power after his evil father, King Ahaz. King Ahaz was one who "provoked the Lord to anger" (2 Chronicles 28:22-26).

Read 2 Chronicles 29:1-8.

1. Describe the character of King Hezekiah:

____

____

2. What was his first order of business upon taking the throne?

____

____

At the time of King Hezekiah's reign, the 12 tribes had been divided into two kingdoms, Israel and Judah. Hezekiah ruled over the southern kingdom, which included the tribes of Judah and part of Benjamin (the greater part of Simon eventually affiliated with Judah). Syria had already taken the Northern Kingdom, Israel, captive.

Read 2 Chronicles 30:1-5.

3. In what month did they celebrate the Passover, and why?

____

____

____

Read 2 Chronicles 30:13-23.

4. What did they do before they sacrificed the Passover lambs?

____

____

5. What happened to those who were unconsecrated, but ate the Passover anyway (vv. 18-19)?

____

____

6. What happened after the seven days of Unleavened Bread (v. 23)?

____

____

7. Name at least three things that happened during this feast that are normally not acceptable. You may want to consult Exodus 12:15-20 and Numbers 9:6-11.

A.____
B.____
C.____

While provisions were made in Numbers 9:6-11 for celebrating Passover in the second month by unconsecrated people, this particular celebration seems to fly in the face of the strict interpretation of the Torah. One could imagine the reaction from the Jewish leaders at the time of Christ. They may have been saying something similar to "The law does not allow for that. I don't care if you are fervently seeking God, follow the rules!" Christian churches today would tend to side with the Pharisees who may have sounded something like "We have never done it like that before. I don't care if you felt the presence of God in the midst of your worship; the temple service can only last one hour. You cannot praise God beyond the time limits!"

We heard a funny story once of a lady in a very conservative church. She began loudly affirming the preacher with "Amen!" and "Praise the Lord!" while he was speaking. One of the elders of the church quietly asked her to control herself. "I can't help it," she said, "I've got joy in my heart!" The elder replied, "Well, you didn't get it here."

8. How did God receive this celebration of Unleavened Bread even though the rules were not followed exactly (2 Chronicles 30:25-27)?

____

____

In this account, we get a glimpse of what is revealed in the New Testament: God is after the heart and the spirit of the law more than the letter of the law. Despite the "rule breaking," this Feast of Unleavened Bread was pleasing to God. We can conclude that God's grace allows for much freedom within a framework of order. How often do we get caught up in the legalism of our own expectations, when we could be celebrating joy at what the Lord has already done for us and anticipating the excitement of what He will do next?

The success of this feast is summed up in 2 Chronicles 30:26, "So there was great joy in Jerusalem, because there was nothing like this in Jerusalem since the days of Solomon the son of David, King of Israel. Then the Levitical priests arose and blessed the people; and their voice was heard and their prayer came to His holy dwelling place, to heaven."

9. What did the Israelites do immediately after the feast (2 Chronicles 31:1)?

____

____

10. What does this tell us about the condition of their hearts?

____

____

When our hearts are right with God, revival takes place. These people, corporately, were moved to action that positively affected their nation because of the revival in their heart. Unfortunately, throughout the following centuries, Israel's obedience to God waxed and waned, ultimately bringing them to miss their Messiah and to lose their temple and their country.

The second temple was destroyed in 70 A.D. This changed the way the Jews celebrate these feasts. They no longer have a temple in which to sacrifice, and they are no longer required to travel to Jerusalem to celebrate the feasts. However; a great deal of preparation still takes place preceding the Feast of Unleavened Bread. To understand more about the preparations, we need to know something about the dietary laws of the Jewish people. God sets up these rules in Leviticus 11, and they are repeated in Deuteronomy 14.

Read Deuteronomy 14:1-21.

11. What is the basic rule for determining if a land animal is clean (v. 7)?

____

12. What determines if a water animal is clean (v. 9)?

____

____

13. What restriction does verse 21 place on the Israelites?

____

____

14. Why do you think the Israelites were given these laws?

____

____

The Jewish kosher laws may seem rather cumbersome, but these laws, through the ages, served both to help keep the people free from disease and to help separate them as a people. Following these meat laws is fairly easy if you purchase all your meat from a kosher butcher. This ensures that only kosher animals are butchered and that they are killed in the appropriate manner. However, the dietary restrictions also include separation of dairy and meat products. This comes from Deuteronomy 14:21. The rabbis have extended the prohibition of boiling a kid in its mother's milk into a prohibition from serving dairy and meat dishes together. Therefore, Jewish households have two separate sets of dishes, including all cooking and serving items, one set for meals cooked with meat and one for those cooked with milk products. Some households even have two dishwashers for each set of dishes!

At Passover, the regular, everyday sets of dishes are put away, and two sets of Passover dishes are used. Since these dishes are only used at Passover, they have never touched food with leaven. Any other needed cooking utensils can be rendered clean by boiling the items in water. This process is called kashering.

Wouldn't it be great if we were as diligent with our lives, keeping the sin completely separated from all we do and think? As hard as we might try, this would be ultimately impossible to do perfectly. Thankfully, the Lord has provided a way for us to be clean through His blood that was shed for us, and even if sin creeps back in, when we humble ourselves and repent, His grace is always sufficient to cleanse our sin from us.

REMEMBERING GOD'S COMMANDS

Read Exodus 13:1-16.

1. Where was the "sign" of Unleavened Bread to be observed from verses 9 and 16?

____

2. Why were they supposed to do this?

____

Exodus 13:1-16 is the basis for Jewish men wearing phylacteries or tefillin (t'FILL-in). The word tefillin comes from a Hebrew word for prayer: "tefilah." Jews wear these prayer boxes as a reminder of the presence of the Lord, His commandments, and their duty to serve the Lord. Four sections of scripture are included in the tefillin. Two of these are Exodus 13:1-10 and Exodus 13:11-16, which we just read. The other two segments of scripture are Deuteronomy 6:4-9, and Deuteronomy 11:13-21. The boxes are worn during prayer, on the head and arm, as prescribed in the above passages.

These boxes serve as capsule-sized reminders of the whole Torah. The leather straps, boxes and parchment are made from kosher animals.

The writing must be handwritten by a scribe. One is worn on the non-dominant hand, then wrapped seven times, and the other is placed on the head, above the hairline on bare skin or hair, not over clothing. Boys do not wear tefillin until their bar-mitzvah, and tefillin are not worn on Sabbaths or festivals. This is because they are to serve as a symbol of God's covenant with Israel. The Sabbaths and festivals are also symbols of that, and so it would be redundant to have two symbols for the same thing on the same day. Tefillin are not even to be handled on Sabbath.

Just as the tefillin are worn, one way to keep God's laws in the forefront of our minds and within easy reach of our hands is by reading God's word and memorizing it. When we memorize scripture, it is within easy access and useful for a ready answer for the hope we possess or to encourage our trust and faith in God during times of need. If you never have, give memorizing scripture a try! It is amazing how "hiding God's word" in your heart can lessen confusion and strengthen your confidence to live under the blessing of His promises. You might try posting a verse in several places around your home as you're working on memorizing it. In fact, a similar idea originated with God in the book of Deuteronomy, as we'll see in these next verses.

Read Deuteronomy 6:4-9.

3. In addition to binding the law to their hand and forehead, where else were they commanded to write them?

____

The Jews still practice this today. They write Deuteronomy 6:4-9 and Deuteronomy 11:13-21 on a scroll of parchment and insert the scroll into a mezuzah case. Mezuzah is a Hebrew word meaning doorpost. It is attached to the doorpost of each entrance to their homes. Some Jews also attach it to the entrance to each interior room (except for such rooms as bathrooms and closets). Interestingly, it is not looked upon as a lucky charm. A mezuzah is simply a reminder upon entering and leaving of the duty to the Torah and all its laws, as well as a reminder of their nation's commitment to worship the one true God.

When we visited Israel a number of years ago, we were somewhat nervous about the trip. We left our three small children at home with relatives. And travel, in general, always seems to bring a higher level of safety concerns. Dallas was reading through the Bible in chronological order at the time, so the portions of scripture were not necessarily arranged by chapter in numerical order. The day before we left, her reading was from Psalm 121, which included great comfort in such verses as 3 and 4, "He will not allow your foot to slip; He who keeps you will not slumber. Behold, He who keeps Israel will neither slumber nor sleep." And verse 8, "The Lord will guard your going out and your coming in from this time forth and forever."

As we traveled throughout Israel, we noticed the mezuzahs on every hotel room where we stayed and were thankful to be reminded that the Lord was watching over our going out and our coming in. Preparing to leave Jerusalem on our last day in Israel, Dallas' scripture reading had come back around to Psalm 122, "I was glad when they said to me, 'Let us go to the house of the Lord.' Our feet are standing within your gates, O Jerusalem."

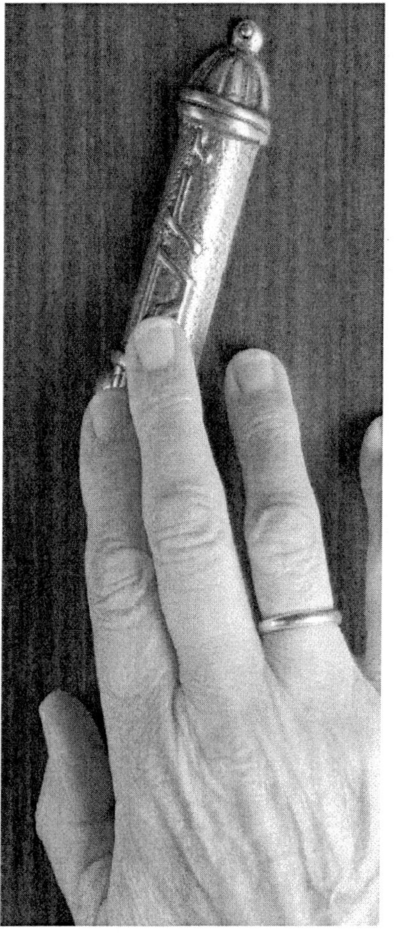

Yes, we were so glad we trusted God to watch over our journey! We were blessed that He reminded us with mezuzahs throughout the journey that He was watching over our coming and going. And our faith was strengthened as we saw the timing and detail of His scripture speak to us in our daily lives, even to the exact geographical location of where our feet were standing on those particular days!

4. How can you apply Deuteronomy 6:4-9 to your life? Rewrite this verse in your own words.

____

____

____

____

____

Deuteronomy 6:4-9 is known to the Jews as the Shema or Sh'ma (emphasis on "ma"). Jewish custom requires a recitation of the Sh'ma every morning and night. It is basically a declaration of faith for the Jewish people.

Read Numbers 15:38-41.

5. What were the Israelites commanded to put on their garments?

____

6. Why were they commanded to do this?

____

____

A talith (a four-cornered prayer shawl) with the required tzitzit (fringes) is traditionally worn by men during morning prayers. Its design varies from elaborate to plain, colorful to embroidered, but it must be four-cornered and have tzitzit. Some Jews wear a small talith all day. It fits over their shoulders and is usually worn under their shirt. While the specific instructions about tying the talith are not found in the Torah, oral tradition has passed along quite a few details and symbolic meaning. Rabbi Hayim Halevy Donin in his book *To Be a Jew*, (Basic Books, 1972, p. 159) cites one of these meanings: "For example, the thirty-nine windings that go into the making of each of the four fringes equal the numerical value of the Hebrew words for "The Lord is One.'"

It is also interesting to note that the current Israeli flag is fashioned after a prayer shawl (talith). During the first Zionist Congress in Basle in 1897, leaders discussed various scenarios for a Zionist flag. It was at that meeting that David Wolffsohn is said to have remarked,

> "What flag would we hang in the Congress Hall? Then an idea struck me. We have a flag - and it is blue and white. The talith (prayer shawl) with which we wrap ourselves when we pray: That is our symbol. Let us take this Talith from its bag and unroll it before the eyes of Israel and the eyes of all nations. So I ordered a blue and

white flag with the Shield of David painted on it. That is how the national flag, that flew over Congress Hall, came into being" (Mishory, 2010).

This statement was made some 51 years before there was a recognized country of Israel! While Wolffsohn probably thought he was being quite original, he was outdone by over 2000 years by the prophet Isaiah. Consider these portions from Isaiah 11:10-12, "Then it will come about in that day that the nations will resort to the root of Jesse, who will stand as a signal for the peoples; … and He will lift up a standard for the nations and will assemble the banished ones of Israel and will gather the dispersed of Judah from the four corners of the earth."

We see this prophecy as a reference to Jesus as the Messiah. He was from the tribe of Judah, more specifically, from the root of Jesse, King David, and He will stand one day as the King of Kings of all nations and will be the ultimate fulfillment of this prophecy. In addition, though, it is notable that there is a literal flag flying over Israel, fashioned after a prayer shawl, a standard for the nations that bears the actual Star of David, and it is gathering the dispersed Jewish people home to Israel in this very time period. It is such a validation of our faith to see that God's word is true, is still coming true, and is relevant in our world today!

Read Matthew 23:1-6.

7. Were the Jews in Jesus' day wearing phylacteries and prayer shawls with fringes?

____

8. Do you believe Jesus thought the Scribes and Pharisees were wrong in wearing these? Give a reason for your answer.

____

____

9. Do you think Jesus wore phylacteries and/or a prayer shawl? Why or why not? (Read Mathew 9:20-21 and Matthew 14:36 for insight on this question).

____

The word for "fringe" used in these verses is kras´-ped-on; meaning fringe or tassel: border, or hem (Zodhiates, 1992). In Mark 5:25-34, a woman touches Jesus' garment and is healed. It was probably this tassel or hem that she touched. Oh, in faith, that we would just reach for the hem of Jesus and reap all the blessings of healing as well!

Jesus wasn't upset with the scribes and Pharisees for wearing the prayer shawl or tefillin. It appears that He wore them Himself. However, their motive was impure, and they seemed to have an attitude of pompous arrogance. We know that tefillin were present during Jesus' time because some of them were found with the Dead Sea scrolls dating back to that time period in the caves at Qumran, Israel, during 1947-1956 (Pearlman, 1988).

We don't often think of Jesus wearing tefillin or covering Himself with a prayer shawl, or touching a mezuzah as He entered His home, but these were the means by which God asked His people to remember Him. Jesus followed these laws with pure motives and not with the intention of calling attention to Himself. God asks us as well to remember Him in every aspect of our lives: our clothing choices, our homes, our thoughts, our prayers, our conversations.

10. Take time to consider actions or habits you may have that are only "for show" rather than for bringing glory to God. Then write down some ways you can actively allow God to permeate every facet of your life.

____

____

____

Redeeming love

We have learned about the origins of the phylacteries and the mezuzah and God's intent for us to remember Him and His word. Exodus 13:1-16 tied these traditions to the Feast of Unleavened Bread. These verses also contain a stipulation about the firstborn and God's intention for them.

Read Numbers 8:13-20.

1. Who does the firstborn male belong to (v. 17)?

____

2. Why (v. 17)?

____

____

3. Who has been taken in place of every firstborn?

____

Read Numbers 18:15-17.

4. What was the redemption price?

___

We see an example of a family not redeeming their firstborn son in 1 Samuel 1. Hannah prayed for a son and made a vow to "give him to the LORD all the days of his life." In this story, she does not redeem her son because he is devoted to the service of the Lord. Had she not dedicated him to the Lord, she would have redeemed him with five silver shekels. Samuel, Hannah's son, goes on to serve as the last Judge of Israel and anoints Saul as the first King of Israel. Samuel also anoints David as the successor to King Saul.

Read Luke 2:21-24.

5. Why did Mary and Joseph bring Jesus to Jerusalem (v. 22)?

___

___

6. What sacrifice did they offer?

___

7. What was this sacrifice for (Leviticus 12:6-8)?

___

___

8. There is no mention that Mary or Joseph paid five shekels, as required, to redeem their firstborn son. Do you think Jesus was redeemed? Why or why not?

___

___

___

___

There are several defenses for both sides of the argument of whether or not Mary and Joseph redeemed Jesus. Let's start with reasons for Jesus' redemption:

1) Jesus did not stay at the temple as did Samuel.

2) Luke 2:39 says, "When they had performed everything according to the law … they returned to Nazareth." This would indicate that they paid the redemption price according to the law and then returned as a family to Nazareth.

Reasons against:

1) Redeeming of a son is more important than the purification of the mother, so it seems that this event would have been recorded if they had redeemed Jesus with five shekels.

2) Luke 2:23 refers to Exodus 13:2, that "Every firstborn male … shall be called holy to the Lord" instead of "must be redeemed."

3) Luke 2:22 says they came to Jerusalem to present him to the Lord, not to redeem him.

4) God is Jesus' Father. The father is responsible for redeeming the child in Jewish law. The next time we see Jesus is when he is in Jerusalem after Passover. In Luke 2:49, it says, "Did you not know that I had to be in My Father's house?" Why would Jesus be redeemed from service to God the Father? His whole purpose was to come in fulfillment of the Old Testament prophecies and to be God's promised Messiah.

The idea of redemption is a central tenet in both Jewish and Christian theology. Redeeming something usually involves a temporary sacrifice ultimately resulting in a permanent gain. We typically think of this as a sacrifice on our part. The sacrifice could be a small task like sticking little green stamps in a booklet to redeem for a cherished prize, or it may be more overwhelming, such as giving up a part of your income or possessions, but the payoff is always worth it. We will see how the Israelites responded to giving over their possessions as we study the Feast of First Fruits in the next chapter. For Hannah and Mary, the sacrifice involved giving up a son for the Lord's service. All of these involve us doing the sacrificing.

When we consider Jesus redeeming us, though, the giving and receiving is reversed. Jesus made the sacrifice. He gave up His life in order to redeem you. You are the payoff! You are what God wanted. You are the prized possession, the permanent gain, the cherished treasure worth redeeming! Jesus paid the price to redeem us by His sinless sacrifice on the cross as payment for our sin. His love redeemed us!

9. What details of how Jesus fits into God's Old Testament plan have impressed you so far in this study?

___

___

Read Mary's prayer in Luke 1:46-56. Take time to offer your own prayer of thanksgiving for God's intricate plan to redeem us through Jesus.

___

___

___

___

While it is important for us to remember God's commands and to strive to put away impure motives and showy arrogance, we cannot remove all of the leaven (sin) from our own lives. However, just like redeeming the green stamps for something far more valuable than a sticky piece of paper, if we confess our sin, reaching out in repentance for the hem of our sinless Savior, His redeeming love removes our sin and gives us grace. His grace showers down upon us in the aftermath of life's floods and is valuable and sufficient for all of our needs. What a great Redeemer!

CHAPTER FIVE

FEAST OF FIRST FRUITS
(First Harvest)

— *A Lesson on Attitudes*

Remember the ad slogan, "Have a Coke and a smile?" Dallas' daddy had both. He was fun to be around, loved young people and football, and owned a grocery store with the biggest candy aisle in town. The candy aisle brought the local high school football players into the store, but Daddy's smiling offer of a free Coke kept those boys hanging around talking to him about football and life. He loved hearing about the next game, the tough workouts, and their chances for making the play-offs. He encouraged them and rooted for them on and off the field. Since he had only daughters, listening to those boys' football stories over a free Coke was a slice of heaven for him. They appreciated his support and wisdom in response.

Two months before he died of cancer, the football players voted him as their "Fan of the Week," inviting him to stand on the sidelines with them and cheer them on. What a great time he had down there clapping and high-fiving and being in on the sideline chatter! More than twenty years after his death, Dallas still meets people who tell her that her dad had a great influence on their life. And that he used to give them a free Coke!

A free soft drink wasn't the only thing her dad gave away. He would frequently let people charge their groceries, knowing they could never repay him, even when the store itself was barely making it financially. He just couldn't stand the thought of denying someone food if it was within his means to help them. A sack of groceries or a free Coke was an easy thing to give away. It didn't cost him much; it wasn't a sacrificial gift by any means, but it was given with a smile. He gave out of his abundance with a big-hearted, happy attitude. In return, he had loyal friends, was held in great respect, and developed relationships that allowed him to share the generous love of his Savior with friends of all ages.

In this section on the Feast of First Fruits, we are going to see that God asks us to give back to Him the first portion of what we've been given. Like Dallas' dad, we always receive so much more in return for even our small gifts. As you learn about this feast, keep in mind what God may be calling you to give out of your abundance. It may be a talent or a gift you have to offer. It may be your finances, your time, or maybe just sharing a soft drink with a friend. We will also discover God's desire for us to give with a right attitude: willingly, generously, and expectantly back to Him. We guess you could say that even God would like a Coke and a smile!

An Attitude of Gratefulness

While the common name for this feast in modern translations is the Feast of First Fruits, the Hebrew Bible more correctly translates this feast as the Feast of First Harvest. This seems a simple detail, but the difference in this more accurate translation of First Harvest is that it indicates a promise and gives hope that there will, in fact, be a full harvest of the year's crop.

Read Leviticus 23:9-14.

1. When were the Israelites supposed to start observing First Fruits (v. 10)?

____

____

2. On what day were the Israelites supposed to observe this feast (v. 11)?

____

____

This feast happens the day after the Sabbath, which we know as Sunday, during the week of Unleavened Bread. The Israelites brought a first portion of their barley harvest — the first spring crop — to the temple as an offering on this day. Through this sacrificial and symbolic act, they were trusting for a bountiful harvest to follow. While the promise of a harvest was given, the Hebrew people still had to wait for the yield, stretching their faith on the one hand, while trusting in God's faithfulness on the other.

The amazing thing is that these instructions were given to them while they were wandering in the desert. If God wanted them to bring a portion of their harvest to Him, it is logical to reason that there must be a fruitful harvest planned for them. Absolutely foundational to trusting God — for them and us — is the knowledge that God's character is one of hope and kindness and provision. Through the establishment of this feast, He encourages the Israelites that He will provide for them in this new and unknown place He is taking them. It isn't hard to imagine that the concept of first fruits also reminded the Israelites of the time when He asked their forefather Abraham to sacrifice his only son (his "first fruits"). As you proceed in this study, you'll consistently see beautiful pictures and examples of how God's character and ways are consistent and good - through the ages and generations. How often are we afraid (or tempted to be afraid) of the future? And yet, God's very nature, from as far back as the time of Moses, and even Abraham, is to protect and to provide for His people and to give them hope.

Our sweet friend, Callie, spent a year in college, close to home, in familiar surroundings, and on a great scholarship. But she just couldn't turn down the gentle nudging to pursue her passion, and she experienced God's provision as she stepped out in obedience to what she felt was God's leading. Leaving behind a college scholarship close to home, she transferred to a university that was far from home, but offered a degree in Christian music ministry, which she felt called to do. The move was a financial and emotional sacrifice for her and her family.

Within hours of her parents dropping her off, Callie had a flat tire on her car. Upon learning from the tire store that she would need to buy a new tire, which she couldn't afford, she broke down in tears. A lady, also in the store waiting for tires, asked Callie if she could help her. Callie tearfully told the lady of her hope to find a job and attend college far from home. A new friendship was born in the tire store. The lady was the owner of a very successful business and offered Callie a job as her assistant. Callie would quickly find herself in the homes of clients who just happened to be in the music business! Come to think of it, we never did hear about Callie's tire. She may still be driving around on the spare.

God is so good to give us hope. He is creative in His ways He provides for us. He gifts us and asks us to step out in the unknown future to serve Him with our gifts. We may feel like we get a flat tire in return, but His ways are always good. His harvest is always bountiful. Since we, too, are his people, that hope extends to us. Then and now, He was calling his people to bold hope for the future.

3. According to Leviticus 23:11, what was the purpose of this offering?

____

____

As we studied the Feasts of Passover and Unleavened Bread, we learned that those feasts were set up by God for the purpose of remembering. It is worth noting that this feast is for the purpose of being accepted (Lev. 23:11 NASB), or in the words of the New International Version, the significance of this feast is that the offering will be "*accepted on your behalf*" (emphasis added). As you continue in this week's study, keep in mind the purpose for this feast and consider why it may be different from that of Passover and Unleavened Bread.

4. According to Leviticus 23:14, what part of the harvest could they use before the first fruits were offered?

____

Read Deuteronomy 26:1-19.

5. What were the Israelites supposed to bring to the temple on the Feast of First Fruits (v. 2)?

____

6. What types of attitudes do you think God expected the giver to have (vv. 5-14)?

____

____

7. How were the Israelites expected to keep these statutes and ordinances (v. 16)?

____

____

8. In verse 17, the people declared the Lord to be their God and that they "would walk in His ways, keep His statutes, His commandments and His ordinances, and

____

____

9. In return for the people's obedience, what did God declare to them (vv. 18-19)?

____

____

____

10. Why do you think God wanted them to bring Him their first fruits?

____

____

____

It is noteworthy that God would not allow the Israelites to benefit from their harvest until they brought the proper offering: the first fruits. God was not asking the Israelites to offer Him something they did not have. He was going to provide the harvest. In return for this provision, though, He expected them to offer the first portion back to Him. It's fascinating to speculate why God would include this stipulation for not using any of the harvest until the first fruits were offered. Maybe He wanted to develop a character quality of trust and gratitude in His people. Perhaps He knew that, if people were left to their own choice in this matter, they would first use all of the harvest for themselves and none would be left for Him. Possibly, God doesn't want "leftovers," but our very best.

In our study on the Feast of Unleavened Bread, we learned about the idea of redemption when we discussed the question of whether or not Mary and Joseph redeemed Jesus. This first fruits offering seems to be another example of redemption. The full harvest belongs to God, but He allows it to be redeemed by the people for their full use by initially offering the first of it to Him.

In our culture today, we are beginning to hear more frequently the upcoming generation being referred to as the "entitlement generation." Recognizing and thanking the Source of our provision in a way that requires an offering on our part keeps us from feeling and acting entitled.

So, in this day and age, what's our offering? According to the words of Jesus, it is nothing less than our life. Jesus said in Luke 9:24, "For whoever wishes to save his life shall lose it, but whoever loses his life for My sake, he is the one who will save it."

In exchange for a pitiful life lived in the desert, maybe what God had in mind for the Israelites and for us is a life of gratefulness, not insistence; of acceptance, not entitlement; of redemption and contentment, not slavery and boredom. God has redeemed us with His Son, the "first fruits of those who have fallen asleep" (1 Corinthians 15). The Israelites offered the very best first so that they could use and enjoy all the full harvest that was left. God offered His best first. He gave His Son so that He could use and enjoy all of us. We are God's harvest. Are you allowing Him to use you? Does it encourage you to think that God *enjoys* you?

As the time for the Feast of First Fruits (First Harvest) approached, the Israelites would begin to watch for the first ripening of their crop. The sheaves of barley that were first to mature, and that represented the best of their yield, were marked as the offering to be taken to the temple. To gather the first harvest of their crop required some amount of trust on the Israelites' part. There was no promise that after the reaping of this first offering, the rest might not be hailed out or devoured by locusts or devastated by some other catastrophic event before it could be harvested. In offering this first harvest, they were putting their confidence in God and His faithfulness to keep His promise of providing a bountiful harvest.

In Biblical times, the economy was based primarily on agriculture, and the word "harvest" had a definite meaning concerning crops. Today, we have many different talents, abilities, and occupations we can offer God.

11. What specific activities, gifts, skills, financial blessings, etc. in your life do you consider your crop to harvest?

____

____

You are God's treasured possession! Take time to listen to God's voice today. Take a moment to check the attitude with which you may be offering some of your "first fruits" and what you may still be holding onto from your "harvest."

12. In accordance with a grateful attitude, what would you be willing to offer Him as the "first fruits of your harvest"?

____

AN ATTITUDE OF EXPECTANCY

The Bible does not give a specific date for celebrating the Feast of First Fruits. Moses is instructed to observe this feast on "the day after the Sabbath." Remember that on the first and last days of the Feast of Unleavened Bread no work was to be done (Leviticus 23:7-8). Any day on which work is prohibited, is referred to as a Sabbath.

In Jesus' time, there was disagreement as to when to celebrate the Feast of First Fruits. The Sadducees understood this Sabbath as the weekly Sabbath (Saturday). This would make the feast celebrated on the first day of the week (Sunday) every year. However, the Pharisees believed that the Sabbath referred to the first day of Unleavened Bread (a high Sabbath). The opinion of the Pharisees was that the feast should be celebrated on the 16th of Nissan, the day after the first day of Unleavened Bread. Celebrating First Fruits on the 16th of Nissan causes the feast to land on a different day of the week each year. Over time, the opinion of the Pharisees was accepted and the 16th of Nissan was considered to be the appropriate date for the feast. However, we will see below that the Sadducees probably had it right all along.

Jews no longer typically celebrate the Feast of First Fruits. The only remaining significance of this feast for Jews is based on Leviticus 23:15-16, which reads, "You shall also count for yourselves from the day after the sabbath, from the day when you brought in the sheaf of the wave offering; there shall be seven complete sabbaths. 'You shall count fifty days to the day after the seventh sabbath; then you shall present a new grain offering to the LORD."

The Feast of First Fruits is used to set the date for celebrating the Feast of Weeks. From evaluating the passage above, we think it is probable that the Sadducees had the correct view after all. First Fruits should fall on the day after the Sabbath (which would be Sunday) during the week of Unleavened Bread. That allows the next feast to always occur on a Sunday (the day after the seventh Sabbath), as the verse above states. We'll learn more about the Feast of Weeks in the next chapter.

The Christian church celebrates the resurrection of Jesus on Easter (the day after the weekly Sabbath during the Feast of Unleavened Bread). This holiday always falls on a Sunday and usually the Sunday after Passover. Consequently, the Feast of Weeks (Pentecost) always falls on a Sunday. So, today's church has taken the Sadducees' view, while current Jews still follow the Pharisees' view.

THE MONTH OF NISSAN-WEEK OF UNLEAVENED BREAD EXAMPLE

Sun	Mon	Tue	Wed	Thu	Fri	Sat
10 Pick out lamb (Palm Sunday)	**11**	**12**	**13**	**14** Passover	**15** Unleavened Bread begins (High Sabbath)	**16** First Fruits Pharisees' view (Weekly Sabbath)
17 First Fruits Sadduccees' view (Resurrection Sunday)	**18**	**19**	**20** End Unleavened Bread (High Sabbath)	**21**	**22**	**23**

Most of the world, including America, uses a solar calendar. This calendar is based on the solar year of 365 days. Every four years, we add an extra day to February. This leap year is necessary to compensate for the solar year actually being 365 ¼ days long. The Jewish calendar is a solar/lunar calendar. This means that the months are based on the lunar month. Each month starts with the arrival of the New Moon. The Muslim calendar is an example of a pure lunar calendar. This is why Muslim holidays such as Ramadan migrate through all the seasons.

The ordinary Jewish year has 12 months with a total of 354 days. To make up for their year being 11 days shorter than the solar year, the lunar calendar is then adjusted to the solar seasons. On leap years an extra day is added to the 12th month (Adar), and an additional month with 29 days is added (Second Adar). The Jewish calendar is based on a 19 year cycle with leap years added in the 3rd, 6th, 11th, 14th, 17th, and 19th years. Without these leap year corrections, the feast days would migrate through all of the seasons. This would violate God's commandment to celebrate the feast days in their season.

Can you imagine celebrating some of our own holidays during different seasons of the year? Christmas just wouldn't be the same if it occurred in the middle of the summer. On the positive side, Santa wouldn't have to worry about getting burned by the fire in the fireplace if Christmas took place in the summer! Jesting aside, however, with our holidays in sync with the seasons, we enjoy the feelings of expectancy that comes when the air becomes crisp and cool, and the leaves on the trees begin to turn colors. The season is changing, bringing the bountiful holiday of Thanksgiving, with Christmas not far behind. We anticipate the family gatherings, the great food, the holiday music, the hot chocolate. Who wants hot chocolate in the summer?!

God made provisions, even within the calendar, for the Israelites to correctly celebrate their feast days. Because of these calendar provisions, the feasts He set up for the Israelites to follow would be celebrated within their rightful season. One-year-old lambs would be plentiful in the spring for Passover, and the correct grain would be ripe for the harvest just as they entered the promised land, so they could enjoy warm, fresh bread after all those years of manna.

In the first section of this chapter, we learned that the Feast of First Fruits was not to be celebrated until the Israelites entered the land that the Lord had promised them. Their first entrance into the promised land is recorded in Joshua 3 and 4 as the Israelites crossed the Jordan into the "land flowing with milk and honey."

Read Joshua 5:5-12.

1. What feast did the Israelites observe when they entered the land (v. 10)?

____

____

2. What clues from verse 11 suggest that they also observed the Feast of Unleavened Bread?

____

____

If the Israelites observed the Feast of Unleavened Bread as verse 11 suggests by its mention of "unleavened cakes," then they would have also observed the Feast of First Fruits, since it falls on the day after the Sabbath during the week of Unleavened Bread.

We know something about the promised land and its fruit from Numbers 13: 23-27, "Then they came to the valley of Eshcol and from there cut down a branch with a single cluster of grapes; and they carried it on a pole between two men, with some of the pomegranates and the figs … . Thus they told him, and said, 'We went in to the land where you sent us; and it certainly does flow with milk and honey, and this is its fruit."

3. In Joshua 5:12, what happened the day after the Israelites "had eaten some of the produce of the land"?

____

We can't pass up this opportunity to point out a fascinating tidbit about Joshua. "Joshua" means "God is salvation." "Jesus" is the Greek transliteration of the Hebrew word "Yeshua" (Joshua) which means "the Lord is salvation." Isn't it interesting that Joshua led the people into the promised land, just as Jesus (Yeshua or Joshua) leads us to heaven, our "promised land!" God's word is wonderfully intricate. And, what a great reward those "first fruits" of the promised land must have been after 40 years of manna!

4. Recall a time when God has blessed you *after* you have offered Him your "first fruits"?

____

In our earlier years of marriage, we belonged to a church whose membership was primarily college students, medical students, and graduate students in residency training. This combination made for some interesting challenges. The church was not particularly "wealthy" since its primary contributors were students, so the members did the cleaning, the maintenance, the lawn care, and the general upkeep and repairs on the facility. There were also ample opportunities to serve in leadership and teaching positions and many people served in several capacities. This was a special sacrifice because of the incredible time constraints on the students due to their post-graduate and doctoral classes and training.

Because there were so many students, about one-fourth of the church membership graduated and moved away every year, and most of us only intended to be there for four years. As a result, if people visited more than twice, they were generally thought of as new members. People were typically asked to mow or clean or maybe even serve communion the next Sunday after only a few visits. Imagine our surprise when, after attending this church for the third Sunday, we were visited by one of the elders who asked if we would like to clean the church the following Saturday. When we agreed, he gave us the key to the building! After we vacuumed and dusted and cleaned bathrooms, we felt like that church was personally OURS. Toward the end of our first year there, we watched with some trepidation as many of the church leaders moved away. The remaining members were already stretched to capacity serving in so many areas; who was possibly going to be able to take on the vacancies left by those moving?

In the beautiful mosaic that we were blessed to observe each year while we were there, God brought in new members to fill vacant posts. Some of the new people were even more particularly gifted for a specific situation than those who had left. For example, an interior designer moved in just as funds became available to finish decorating the inside of the sanctuary, and a new medical student who was a former pastor moved in, agreeing to help fill the pulpit in the final weeks before a new pastor arrived.

Year after year, God sustained that little church. We began to have an attitude of childlike, eager expectancy as the summer passed and autumn approached. It was akin to waiting for Christmas. For as this little church sent out the first of its harvest (i.e., professionals equipped to be leaders and servants in their next churches) God provided those of us left behind with a fresh, incoming class of excited believers to serve and encourage … and to mow and to clean bathrooms!

Let us live our lives, then, expecting God to provide a great harvest for us so that we may return to Him a plentiful first offering.

AN ATTITUDE OF ACCEPTANCE

As we begin to see the shadow of Christ in the Feast of First Fruits, let's look at some interesting information Jesus tells us before He celebrates His last Passover with the disciples.

Read John 12:20-32.

1. Who were among those going to worship at the Passover (v.20)?

___

The word "Greek" in this passage is from the word "Hellen" meaning a Greek-speaking person, especially a non-Jew, a Gentile (*Spiros Zodhiates*, 1992). In John 12:21-22, Philip and Andrew tell Jesus that some Greeks wish to see Him. Rather than acknowledge this announcement from the disciples, Jesus seems to change the subject.

2. What conclusions can you draw from Jesus' strange response to this information in John 12:23-28?

____

____

____

3. In your own words, what message do you think Jesus is giving to the Gentiles and to His disciples in John 12:24?

____

____

4. What "purpose" or "reason" do you think Jesus was talking about in John 12:27?

____

____

5. In verse 32, whom does Jesus say will be drawn to Him?

____

It seems that once the Greeks begin seeking Jesus, the time has finally come to draw all men, Jew and Gentile alike, unto Himself. In the Feast of Passover, we saw Jesus as the Lamb of God, sacrificed for us on the day the feast was celebrated. He took on our sin (leaven) and had to be hidden away on the very day of Unleavened Bread. Consider how Jesus fulfills the Feast of First Fruits.

Read Luke 23:54-24:9.

6. What did Jesus do on His last Feast of First Fruits (the day after the Sabbath or Sunday), while Israel was bringing a portion of the first of their harvest before the Lord?

____

____

Read I Corinthians 15:20-23 and Revelation 1:5.

7. How is Christ described?

____

____

8. From Revelation 1:5, of what do you think Christ was a "faithful witness"?

____

____

Read Matthew 27:50-53.

9. Why do you think there were other people raised from the dead after the resurrection of Jesus?

____

Jesus rose from the dead on the Feast of First Fruits and became the firstborn of the dead. The day after Sabbath is Sunday. This particular day after Sabbath is what we know as Easter Sunday. This God-man, Jesus, is a faithful witness. He gives a true account of what He has seen and heard. He is Truth. He did what He said He would do in conquering death, but He also was a true witness to creation, to the fall of man, to the futility of Satan's power, and to the majesty and authority of the Father.

Because of the Messiah's power over death, Jews and Gentiles alike have the opportunity to be accepted as His children and have life everlasting with Him. We will see this particular theme reiterated in the Feast of Weeks in the next chapter. Jesus was the ultimate Jewish man, keeping all of the law. He was sacrificed as the Lamb of God on Passover, hidden away as leaven on the Feast of Unleavened Bread, and He rose again on the Feast of First Fruits. Maybe He even brought His own first fruits with Him in anticipation of a bountiful harvest of souls to follow. This would explain the other people who were raised from the dead at this same time.

We mentioned earlier that God set up Passover and Unleavened Bread for the Israelites to remember, but the Feast of First Fruits was to be accepted. To *remember* God's love, deliverance, redemption, and sacrifice is the focus of the Passover and Unleavened Bread celebrations. As Christians, we take communion to *remember* these events. However, as we noted earlier, the Feast of First Fruits was for the purpose of being accepted, or that the offering would be accepted on our behalf. We see in this feast that both interpretations of scripture are met. The Feast of First Fruits is a celebration of resurrection, allowing us to be *accepted* into that love and encouraging us to live a life that sows and reaps a bountiful and acceptable harvest. We are accepted because Jesus Christ, the First Fruit, was found *acceptable on our behalf* as the perfect sacrifice.

AN ATTITUDE OF RESURRECTION

Looks of bewilderment and confusion, a suppressed grin — such were the responses from fellow church members last Easter when we cheerfully greeted them with, "Happy First Fruits!" instead of "Happy Easter!" A few people heartily returned our greeting, "Happy First Fruits, indeed!" And one or two deliberately beat us to the punch, greeting us first with "Happy First Fruits!" That made our day!

We had been teaching a group in our church about this feast. Many had heard our conundrum concerning the customary title of Easter given to the observance of Resurrection Sunday. It is commonly known as Easter, but on the morning Jesus rose from the grave, the Jewish nation was busy celebrating the Feast of First Fruits, the God-ordained feast introduced to the Israelites over a thousand years earlier.

In the previous section, we mentioned that Christians recognize the Feast of First Fruits as Easter. While we celebrate Jesus' resurrection on Easter Sunday, wouldn't it be more meaningful if we called it the Feast of First Fruits?! Why do we call it Easter, anyway?

Most likely, Easter was given that name to commemorate a pagan goddess with a similar sounding name of Ishtar. After the destruction of the temple in 586 B.C. by the Babylonians, many of the Israelites were taken captive to Babylon. The Babylonians worshipped many gods and goddesses. One of these was the fertility goddess, Ishtar. She was worshipped for her supposed power to facilitate reproduction. Traditions involving Ishtar included worshipping other things that reproduced quickly, such as bunnies, and playing with and hunting for eggs. After all, reproduction at its simplest form is a hunt for an egg.

When we studied Passover in Chapter 2, we mentioned several items that were on the Seder plate: bitter herbs, charoset, horseradish, a bone, and so forth. However, we only briefly mentioned that there is also a roasted egg on the plate. For the Jewish people, the egg reminds them of the destruction of the temple. They dip the egg in salt water as a symbol of tears and of their sadness over the destruction of the temple. While it's unclear when the egg appeared on the Seder plate, it makes sense that it could have found its way there during, or just after, the captivity under the influence of the Babylonians.

We appreciate and understand the need for the Jews to remember and grieve the loss of the temple at the time of Passover. We can respect that an egg may be an acceptable symbolism for Babylon destroying it. However, we are dismayed that Christians have taken the title of Easter and its emphasis on reproduction instead of the Jewish title, Feast of First Fruits.

We are not celebrating reproduction at Easter. We are celebrating resurrection! It is hope for new life, for everlasting life. We worship a Messiah who has conquered death and has given us life, not through reproduction, but through the power of the resurrection. It's too bad we've come so far from our faith's Jewish roots.

In studying Passover, Unleavened Bread, and First Fruits, we have looked at many passages from the four Gospels. However, we studied most of the verses individually and without the surrounding context. Now let's read through a large part of Jesus' last week on earth as it is recorded in Matthew. See what insight you can find when reading this text with your new understanding of the Feasts of Passover, Unleavened Bread, and First Fruits.

Starting with Matthew 26:1, read to the end of the book of Matthew. Use the space below to record any thoughts, or new insights, you would like to remember as you read this with a Jewish perspective of the feasts and their meanings.

____

____

____

____

____

We hope you are recognizing some of the remarkable ways God set a pattern for Jesus to follow, along with prophecies for Him to fulfill in the Jewish feasts. By the way, anyone know any Babylonians? As a people, they did indeed cease to exist. Reproduction wasn't the key to eternal life. Resurrection is! We serve a resurrected Savior, Christ the First Fruits. Maybe this spring, you will wish everyone a "Happy First Fruits!"

CHAPTER SIX

FEAST OF WEEKS (Shavuot)

— *A Lesson in Provision*

Would you believe God can use a blue sleeping bag? We recently took a trip to Dallas, Texas. Carl was traveling on, but Dallas was staying in the area, so she rented a car for her time in the city. We, along with our daughter, Paris, went to pick up the rental car. On the way, Paris stuck a part of a blue sleeping bag out the window to keep the sun out of her face. Dallas picked up the rental car, and Carl agreed to lead her back to the particular highway she needed before their roads parted.

Dallas was very nervous driving a brand new, rented car in afternoon traffic in a big city. As we pulled out of the rental parking area, she tried to get Paris' attention to take the sleeping bag out of the window. It was sticking out pretty far and flapping against the outside of the car. Paris didn't see her, though, and we continued out into the traffic. Dallas took great care to stay on Carl's bumper as she followed through the thick traffic. However, we were quickly separated, and while she couldn't spot the actual car, she could see the blue sleeping bag just past the edge of the semi-truck in front of her. The sleeping bag was waving wildly, as if yelling, "Follow me! Follow me!"

Carl was slowing to let cars go around. Dallas found herself behind him just barely in time to see him signal her over as he exited off the other way. She immediately felt so alone, cut off from the one who loved her and had taken care of her to that point on the trip. The instant after Dallas felt that loneliness, she felt a rush of comfort, and the thought came to her mind, *"But you're never cut off from ME. I'm the One who loves you and provides for you."* And she thanked God for His provision of the blue sleeping bag that He had prepared ahead of time just for her — even before she knew she needed it.

GOD PROVIDES THE LAW

Pentecost is the one Jewish feast with which the Christian church has some familiarity. "Pente" is Greek for fifty, and the name Pentecost literally means "the fiftieth day." This feast comes fifty days after the Sabbath after Passover. The word "Pentecost" is not found in the Old Testament, but it is used three times in the New Testament to refer to this feast. The book of Acts tells us that the apostles were gathered together for the Feast of Pentecost, also called the Feast of Weeks, or "Shavuot."

Shavuot (shuh-VOO-oht) is a Hebrew word meaning "weeks," for God set up this feast seven weeks after that of First Fruits. It is at the Feast of Weeks, which the Jewish nation had been celebrating for about 1,500 years before the time period when Jesus was crucified, that the Holy Spirit descended upon the apostles. In the Christian church, we usually assume that the giving of the Holy Spirit at this time is what began the celebration of Pentecost, but in reality, the giving of the Holy Spirit was the fulfillment of a feast that was set up by God in Leviticus 23, long before this particular Christian event took place and was recorded in the Book of Acts.

As we studied in the last chapter, the Feast of First Fruits was, and is still today, the day for the Jewish nation to begin "counting the omer." An omer is a unit of measure equal to about half of a gallon, and the nation literally counts down the fifty days until this next feast of Shavuot. Later in this chapter, we will see exactly what the disciples were doing during the counting of the omer.

Read Leviticus 23:15-22.

1. How much time elapses from the Feast of First Fruits until this feast? In number of weeks: ____________ In number of days: ____________

2. What is the first offering mentioned?

____

3. What is different about these loaves compared with the bread in the previous three feasts?

____

The Feast of Weeks, or Pentecost, originally celebrated the beginning of the long summer wheat harvest. As we read in Leviticus 23, it was commanded that a grain offering be brought to the temple. This grain offering was to be two loaves of bread made from fine flour and leaven. These leavened loaves were then brought to the temple and waved before the altar as an offering to the Lord. This is a significant change, since all of the prior feasts used unleavened bread. As you continue through this chapter, consider what these loaves might represent.

4. Deuteronomy 16:9-12 outlines the features of the Feast of Weeks. According to these verses, who was included in the celebration of this feast?

____

____

5. Why were they supposed to keep this feast?

____

____

Since the destruction of the temple in 70 A.D., Shavuot, or Pentecost, changed from a feast celebrating the beginning of the summer agricultural harvest to a time of remembering the giving of the law at Mt. Sinai. While the Bible makes no association between Shavuot and the events at Mt. Sinai, the Talmud does make a connection between the two. Because of the temple destruction, people couldn't bring their loaves and offerings to the temple anymore, so the rabbis shifted the focus for this holiday after calculating a correlation on the calendar between the season of this feast and the season of the events that took place on Mt. Sinai.

Read the account of the giving of the law in Exodus, Chapter 32.

6. What were the people doing while Moses was on the mountain?

____

____

7. In Exodus 32:5, it says, "Tomorrow shall be a feast to the Lord." If there was supposed to be a feast anyway, what do you think was so bad about the golden calf?

____

8. What did God want to do to them in verse 10?

____

9. Who was "for the Lord" in verse 26?

____

10. How many* people were killed in verse 28?

____

**Note: This number will be significant later in the study.*

Read Exodus 34:1, 29-35.

11. What happened to Moses' face?

____

12. Why?

____

____

13. What did Moses do when he finished speaking to the people (v. 33)?

____

____

While the people were still under Pharaoh's rule in Egypt, Moses asked Pharaoh to let his people go because they needed to make a sacrifice to their God in the desert. The Hebrew people surely expected to take part in this sacrifice. In Exodus 32:5, when they are told that a feast of the Lord will be "tomorrow," it is reasonable to see how they twisted the command and the motive to fit their own needs. They took advantage of what God meant for good, created a "feast" of their own, and distorted the worshiping of the Lord. Out of the selfishness of their hearts, they worshiped a golden calf while participating in unacceptable, inappropriate behavior. Moses, however, was in the presence of the Lord and focusing on God's commands so much that his very face glowed.

14. What plans have you made that will put you in the presence of God on a daily basis?

____

____

We read Exodus 32 and then skipped to chapter 34. In Chapter 33, the people repent. Moses seeks God's glory and prays for favor in God's sight for himself and for his nation. He also prays that they may be distinguished from all other people on earth. If Moses really knew what he was asking, he might take that last part back. The Jews are, to this day, distinguished from other people. However, Moses probably did not have in mind the persecution, anti-Semitism, dispersions, or holocaust that played a part in answering that prayer. Of course, God distinguished them from all the peoples on the earth in positive ways, too: their dietary laws and obedience to the moral codes in the law kept them healthier and better off than many of the less civilized cultures around them. Also, as the chosen people of God, they became a great kingdom under God-fearing kings like David and Solomon. In addition, God gave the Israelites upright judges and the prophets; He provided a Messiah to them as he had promised. Through many dark ages down to the modern era, there have been thinkers, scientists, and business leaders who were from the Jewish people and achieved prominence and blessing; and the Jews, as a whole, have maintained their unique culture intact probably unlike any other culture in history has been able to do. They obtained the blessings that come from living out morality based on God's truth. There seems to be a principle here: that as believers in God, there will be great persecution along with great suffering, but also abundant blessing. One of those blessings for the Jewish people is the gift of the Torah.

Because the Feast of Weeks has come to be known by the Jewish people as a time to commemorate the giving of the Torah, it is referred to in the Jewish prayer book as "*zman matan torateinu*" or the "season of the giving of the Torah." We should understand that the Hebrew word "Torah" is translated into English as "Law," but its true meaning is "instruction" or "teaching." This is significant later in the study — that the Torah is not just a strict set of laws, but it is much more. What a blessing that the God of the Universe would give us a book of instructions!

The Torah is what Christian believers refer to as the Pentateuch, the first five books of the Old Testament: Genesis, Exodus, Leviticus, Numbers, and Deuteronomy. What we call the "Old Testament," Jews call the "Tanakh." The books in the Tanakh are exactly the same as in the Old Testament except the order is different. The Tanakh has the Torah, or the Pentateuch, first, the same order as in the Old Testament.

Then, the Nevi'im, which literally means "prophets," comes after the Torah, and following that is the Kethuvim, which literally means "writings." The word Tanakh is actually a type of acronym for **T**orah, **N**evi'im, and **K**ethuvim. Of course, the Jews would not call the Tanakh the Old Testament, as that would imply there is a new one. Another important book to the Jews is the Talmud. The Talmud is basically a collection of rabbinical commentaries on the Torah.

The Torah as a whole is not all "Law." Genesis is a book of beginnings. It presents the account of creation and tells of the beginning of mankind. It introduces the lineage of the Chosen People and hints at the plan for a Messiah (Genesis 3:15).

Exodus (in Hebrew) means "names," and it is a book of names of the people who exited Egypt with Moses. It's estimated that this group of people numbered about 2.5 million. From such a small clan of 12 brothers, what a tremendous group of people survived, even in the midst of hardship and slavery!

Leviticus was written during the same time period as the book of Exodus and is mostly about how to build and manage a tabernacle for worshiping God. The Levites, in particular, have a distinct set of laws just for them. As we read in Exodus 32, it was the Levites who were "for the Lord" at the giving of the law. Thus, it is appropriate that they are the group that is in charge of the keeping of the tabernacle for the Lord.

Numbers is a book of wanderings and is called "in the wilderness" by the Jews. And then there's Deuteronomy, which means "second law," and in this book Moses essentially recaps the highlights of the law. God has compassion for our forgetfulness, doesn't He? He "knows our weakness" (Psalm 78:39) and as in the case of Deuteronomy, uses repetition to teach His people. He gives us reminders and even repeatedly commands us to remind ourselves and our children of His ways, generation after generation (Deuteronomy 6:4-9).

So, the Torah (the Pentateuch) was never intended to be a code of "do's and don'ts." It serves as a reminder to the people of their history and heritage and also as a collection of God's teachings that help us to understand Him better. It has been called a "who-we-are-and-how-to-live" book. In fact, many of our children's Bible stories come from the Torah: the Garden of Eden, Noah and the Flood, the Hard-Hearted Pharaoh and the Plagues. These so-called children's stories are, in fact, a solid foundation to knowing and loving God! The stories from creation forward show that God is the divine covenant-keeper with people who put their faith in Him. In this sense, "who-we-are-and-how-to-live" seems a fitting description for this section of scripture.

Remember, each feast we are studying points, in some way, to God's provision for our need for a messiah. In the Feast of Weeks, God giving a harvest and the law was another example of His provision for His people. We see our need for a messiah, a savior, by realizing our sin through the law, the Torah.

Paul tells us that the Torah (Law) shows us what sin is. In Romans 7:7, he says, "What shall we say, then? Is the Law sin? May it never be! On the contrary, I would not have come to know sin except through the Law; for I would not have known about coveting if the Law had not said, 'You shall not covet'." If we were given freedom without knowing right from wrong, we would be living as animals. In Deuteronomy 16:12, God tells the people what they are to remember at the Feast of Weeks: "And you shall remember that you were a slave in Egypt, and you shall be careful to observe these statutes."

As Christians, we are reminded that at the first Pentecost after Christ's death, God gave us freedom from the Law through the Holy Spirit. "However, the Law is not of faith; on the contrary, 'He who practices them shall live by them.' Christ redeemed us from the curse of the Law, having become a curse for us — for it is written, 'Cursed is everyone who hangs on a tree' — in order that in Christ Jesus the blessing of Abraham might come to the Gentiles, so that we might receive the promise of the Spirit through faith" (Galatians 3:12-14).

Because the Feast of Weeks is connected to Passover by Counting the Omer, it is viewed as the feast that closes out the Passover season. This is signified by the fact that the Talmud refers to this feast by the name *Atzeret* (which implies a concluding festival). When we study these feasts in the light of Christ, we can see how the feasts of Passover and Weeks are tied closely together. It is God's laws that give meaning to our freedom. And although we're not under the law, we can still use it as a guidebook to lead us to Christ. Also, while Jesus fulfilled the Feasts of Passover, Unleavened Bread, and First Fruits, He did not leave us without a Comforter. The giving of the Spirit at the Feast of Weeks completes the story.

Jesus came as the Lamb to become sin for us, hidden away as leaven, and raised again as the first fruits of the living dead. And at the Feast of Weeks, God poured forth His Spirit so that "everyone who calls on the name of the Lord shall be saved (Acts 2:21)." We need a Savior, and we also need the Spirit poured out on us that we may be continually led by Him and not under the law (Galatians 5:18).

Many Jewish traditions are associated with the Feast of Weeks. One of these is the eating of dairy products as a reminder that the knowledge of the Torah is sweet, like milk and honey under the tongue. Today, it is also traditional for some to stay up all night reading and studying in preparation for the holiday that celebrates the giving of the Torah. They read a portion of scripture from the beginning and end of every major section of the Old Testament. Some sections are read in full, including the books of Ezekiel and Ruth.

Wouldn't it behoove us as Christians to study the Bible equally diligently? The Old Testament, and God's word in general, is absolutely fascinating. There is nothing like it. It interprets itself, and it never contradicts itself. It withstands the test of time and can be studied to infinity.

Many nights, especially when Carl is working the evening shift, Dallas has gone to bed holding her Bible tightly to her chest. She's even kissed it on occasion. She keeps her Bible by her bed and reads it most every night. Sometimes it seems to call out to her. When that happens, she can hardly wait to open it. She knows the Holy Spirit is nudging her to listen to Him by reading His word. It never fails that God has something just for her, some truth, some hope, some timely advice for the exact situation that is plaguing her. God is so wonderful, and His word speaks to us on such a personal and intimate level!

We hope that you, too, learn to love the scriptures as you see how God has placed meaning in the smallest details. Whether it be the Torah, the book of Proverbs, the Psalms, the book of Isaiah, the gospels, or one of the epistles, may you find portions of scripture that become dear to you, so dear that you find comfort in them in the darkest night and receive joy when you start the new day studying them.

In the next section, we are going to take a look at the two books, Ezekiel and Ruth, and their relevance to the Feast of Weeks. You will see, once again, the compassionate provision of a God who has covered everything to give you a hope and a future. You will see the intricate way He foreshadowed in this Jewish feast the otherwise mysterious gift of the Holy Spirit that he eventually gave to the apostles, whose knowledge of the feasts probably helped them recognize God's gift and power that was imparted to them while they were observing the Feast of Weeks, or Pentecost.

GOD PROVIDES A REDEEMER

Read the book of Ruth. (Don't worry, this is a fun story and the whole book is just 4 chapters long. This will only take you about 15 minutes, so take your time and enjoy the read.)

1. What time of year does this story happen? (Ruth 1:22)

____

2. What nationality was Ruth?

____

3. According to Ruth 1:16, did Ruth believe in the God of Israel?

____

We see that the book of Ruth is an appropriate reading for the Feast of Weeks since the story is set during the time frame of the Counting of the Omer. Ruth was a Moabitess, a descendant of Lot, which makes her a Gentile. It is evident in this story that God provides for His people, even the Gentiles. However, because Ruth was a widow with no children, it was necessary for her to be redeemed in order to carry on the Jewish family's name.

4. Read Leviticus 25:47-49. Who could redeem her according to this law?

____

____

5. How was Boaz related to Naomi? (Ruth 2:20)

____

The word for relative here is "goel," which is Hebrew for "kinsman-redeemer."

6. Was Boaz willing to pay the price to purchase Ruth's redemption (Ruth 3:11, 4:9, 10)?

____

We see Boaz as a type (a foreshadowing) of Christ, a kinsman-redeemer. Because Jesus was both God and man, he was both deity and "kin" to us. It's also interesting that Boaz waited for Ruth to ask for redemption, just as we must ask Jesus to redeem us. Furthermore, Boaz was a man of great standing and means available to redeem Ruth; so too, Jesus had the price to redeem us in that he was found worthy as the perfect Lamb of God. And, he was willing. He laid down his life for us. However, just like Ruth, we have to ask. And, after we invite Him into our hearts, Jesus doesn't stop with redemption. He continues to provide for us. Let's consider how God provided for Ruth. Keep in mind that more than 400 years elapse between the writing of Leviticus and the story of Ruth.

Read Leviticus 23:22 with Ruth 2:2.

7. How did God provide for the physical needs of Ruth and Naomi before they were even born?

____

____

8. According to Ruth 4:13-15, how did God further bless them?

____

____

9. What name did Ruth's son have?____________
Who was Obed's grandson?_________
Who descended from David? (2 Timothy 2:8) ___________

In Matthew 1 and Luke 3, we see the genealogies of Christ recorded through His earthly father, Joseph, and his mother Mary. Both sides trace back to David, Jesse, Obed, Boaz, and beyond. This is a beautiful result of a Gentile woman who believed in the God of Israel and was willing to be redeemed by a kinsman-redeemer. We too, being willing, have been redeemed by a kinsman-redeemer and have been grafted-in as the Gentile bride of Christ.

In Ruth 3:9, Ruth asks Boaz to "spread your covering over your maid, for you are a close relative." A custom of that day was to spread a covering over someone to symbolize a pledge to marry. We see God speaking to Jerusalem in Ezekiel 16:8 "'...Then I passed by you and saw you, and behold, you were at the time for love; so I spread My skirt over you and covered your nakedness. I also swore to you and entered into a covenant with you so that you became Mine,' declares the Lord God."

In his book, *Being Jewish*, Ari Goldman speaks of a Jewish tradition that suggests, "Passover is the courtship of the Jews, Shavuot is the wedding, and Sukkot (the festival of booths), is the setting-up of a home together where both — God and Israel — can live" (Goldman, 2000). In addition, there is a tradition of Jews going without sleep the first night of the festival, like a groom standing vigil before his wedding day. So Shavuot, the Feast of Weeks, is a wedding feast of sorts in which the people of Israel are reminded of the joining together of God and bride.

During Shavuot, Sephardic Jews (Jews that originate primarily from Spain) also read a ketubah, a marriage contract between God, the groom, and Israel, the bride. They use the very words that were used on Mount Sinai by the ancient Jews (Exodus19:8), "We will do and we will listen." Blu Greenberg, in her book *How to Run a Traditional Jewish Household*, defines her idea of God's covenant between God and the Jews, "In three thousand years of ups and downs, neither partner has said, 'Enough already.' That's what a covenant is" (Greenberg, 1983, p. 466).

The book of Ruth is an appropriate reading for the Feast of Shavuot (Pentecost) for several reasons:

- It occurs at harvest.
- Ruth, a Gentile, aligned herself with the law.
- Even from the beginning of the law, God made provision through a kinsman-redeemer for Gentiles to be included.
- It is a wedding story, and Jews believe that they are wed to God through the law.

The Feast of Weeks is a "lesser known" Jewish feast when compared to Passover, or the Day of Atonement. According to Greenberg, this festival is "a Jewish housewife's dream. There is no massive house-cleaning, no need to plan and cook for umpteen holiday meals" (Greenberg, 1983, p. 460). One of the favorite preparations is to grab an afternoon nap. This is done because the custom is to stay awake all night to study the Torah. Perhaps by observing this practice, the Jewish people were reminded of the priority the Torah had in their lives.

As we mentioned earlier, it is customary to eat dairy foods on the Feast of Weeks. Along with the dairy foods is served two loaves of bread (*challot*; plural of *challah*) baked with honey. This is also reminiscent of the wave offering of the two leavened loaves offered during this feast as set out in Leviticus 23 — a delicious way to remember what used to be done when there was a temple at which to celebrate! Similar to what is seen at a Jewish wedding, the home and the synagogue are decorated with plants, flowers, and tree branches. This is fitting because the Jews feel that they were "wed" to God at Mt. Sinai. Since the entire Shavuot festival is focused on the giving of the law, it is also traditional for children to begin their study of the Torah at this time.

We saw in our study how God provided for Ruth with the stipulation for gleaning. This extensive list of offerings and animals and holy convocations seemingly interrupted by "Oh, and by the way, don't harvest all your fields to the corners" must have seemed a silly sounding footnote to the laws given concerning the celebration of Shavuot. Yet, God had a plan to take care of Ruth many years in the future. And with the initiation of these feasts, He set in place a shadow of things to come, the substance of which is Christ. He knew people could not keep the law, and so He provided the Messiah. He knew we needed a kinsman-redeemer. He knew we couldn't make it on our own without Him, and so He provided the Spirit, our Comforter.

God knew we were leavened Gentiles. We can't keep the law; our forebears didn't even know what it was! Yet, through Pentecost we see that He provided for us, too, with life in His Son and abundance in His Spirit, before we even knew we needed it. Fortunately, for us, He continues to provide for our every need.

This feast is set up by God to help the people remember all He has done for them. Recall a time when God has provided for you even before you knew you needed it. Perhaps he orchestrated events or a series of events; it may have even involved something like a blue sleeping bag, as in Dallas' story. Maybe He gave you a divine appointment in a way that provided a good or advantageous outcome for you.

____

____

____

____

____

From the initial establishment of the feasts, we see demonstrations and remembrances that God's character is generous. Throughout scripture, He is the giver of "every perfect gift" (James 1:17). Our generous God always looks out for us — before and after the fact. No wonder Romans 8:28 is a favorite of so many of us.

GOD PROVIDES THE HOLY SPIRIT

In our study of Ruth, we established that God's plan included providing even for the Gentiles. In this section, we see God's provision of the Holy Spirit given to the apostles on Pentecost.

Remembering that Christ arose on Feast of First Fruits, read Acts 1:1-5.

1. How many days was Christ with the apostles after His resurrection?

____

2. How many days were between First Fruits and Pentecost?

____

3. How many days was Jesus talking about in Acts 1:5 when He said, "... but you shall be baptized with the Holy Spirit not many days from now ..."?

____

____

We see here what the disciples were doing during the counting of the omer. They spent 40 of those 50 days with the risen Lord. Jesus taught and walked among them during this time until His ascension where He encouraged them to wait in Jerusalem until they would be "clothed with power from on high" (Luke 24:49).

In hindsight, we can see that it was only 10 days until they received this power in the form of the Holy Spirit at the Feast of Weeks. This waiting period must have been tortuous. Were they tempted, as the Israelites had been while waiting 40 days for Moses to come down from the mountain? We wonder if they may have felt somewhat like our daughter did at her high school graduation. When asked how she felt about completing this season of her life she responded, "Now that I'm finally here, I don't know what to do with myself."

How often do we run around so busily trying to accomplish a goal, only to find ourselves at a loss for what to do next when we've finished?! Sometimes we must wait, gather our courage, and wait some more while we seek God's will for the next season of our life.

While the disciples waited, they went back to what they knew. "And they returned to Jerusalem with great joy, and were continually in the temple, praising God" (Luke 24:52-53). Acts 1:12-14 tells us that they were "continually devoting themselves to prayer … " When we wait on God, wouldn't it be wise to go back to what we know is true in scripture and be faithful to it? While sometimes we are simply waiting on God's timing, as long-time Christians, we've often heard it taught that God does not give increased revelation until we act on what He told us to take care of first. This is not always the case, but sometimes we do need to ask the Holy Spirit if the reason we're not moving on in our lives is due to the omission of some work God has told us to do.

Even if you are waiting on God for a breakthrough, what could you do that you know would be faithful to what God has shown you thus far? Spend time in prayer? Spend time in God's word? Give your time to someone who needs help? Attend church services? (Keep in mind the admonition in Hebrews 10:25 to keep gathering with other believers, "not forsaking our own assembling together, as is the habit of some, but encouraging one another … .")

The disciples knew God would not forsake His promise to give them power. And sure enough, the ancient feast of Pentecost turned out to be the jumping off point for their anointing by the Holy Spirit. Today, the Jewish people are still counting the days until the Feast of Weeks. As we noted earlier, the reading of the book of Ruth is a long-held tradition that is observed during that time. Another book traditionally read in full on Shavuot (Pentecost) is Ezekiel.

Read Ezekiel 1:4.

4. What did Ezekiel see?

____

____

5. What was in the cloud?

____

In Acts 2:1-4, read what happened to the disciples as they experienced their first Feast of Weeks without Jesus present.

6. What did the disciples hear?

____

7. What did the disciples see?

____

____

It is interesting to consider the mindset of the apostles. Maybe they had read Ezekiel on the day of this feast many times. Yet now they were experiencing an outpouring of the Holy Spirit that was similar to Ezekiel's vision of God. Just as Jesus fulfilled the first three feasts, to the day, with his death, burial, and resurrection, the Holy Spirit fulfilled the Feast of Weeks to the day. Individuals in the Old Testament had been filled with the Holy Spirit on occasion, but Pentecost marks the first time that the Holy Spirit is given corporately. As the group of believers received the gift of the Holy Spirit, the Christian church was born. Peter preached to the crowd, and about 3,000 people were baptized and added to their number (Acts 2:37-41).

At the southern entrance to the temple, archeologists have found several large ritual baths (called *mikvahs*). It was customary to immerse oneself in these baths for ritualistic purity before entering the temple. These mikvahs were probably where the new believers in Jesus were baptized. With over two million Jews in the city for the Feast of Weeks, it would not have caused a spectacle for 3,000 people to go through a mikvah again. Interesting to note is that the outpouring of the Holy Spirit was a public event much like the giving of the Torah had been a public event at Mt. Sinai. Both of these gifts, the Torah and the Spirit, were for all people who believed. (God is so consistent, isn't He?)

Read Acts 2.

8. Who fulfills this Feast of Weeks that the people have both seen and heard (Acts 2:33)?

____

In the first section of this chapter, we learned that everyone was included in the celebration of Pentecost.

9. According to Acts 2:21 who can be saved?

____

____

10. Who is this promise for (Acts 2:39)?

____

____

11. Recalling Exodus 32:28, how many were killed at the giving of the law? __________ How many were saved with the giving of the Holy Spirit on Pentecost? __________ (Acts 2:41).

12. Write out the last two phrases of 2 Corinthians 3:6.

____

____

____

____

____

____

____

____

____

Once again, God's actions under the old covenant are interpreted, fulfilled, and explained in the New Testament. Unfortunately for Christians, the view of the Torah being a hard set of unforgiving laws is a common one. This unfortunate misconception is conveyed in the classic book *Pilgrim's Progress* by John Bunyan. The main character, Christian, is talking to his fellow pilgrim, Faithful. They are discussing their adventures on the straight and narrow path.

> "**Faithful**: Good brother, listen to me, as soon as he overtook me, it was a word and a blow. He knocked me down in an attempt to kill me. When I came to, I asked him why he treated me like this. He said it was because I was inclined to go with Adam the first. Then he struck me with another deadly blow to my chest knocking me backwards. I lay at his feet as dead. When I regained consciousness, I cried to him for mercy. He said, I do not know how to show mercy and he knocked me down again. He would have killed me, but one came by and ordered him to stop.
>
> **Christian**: Who ordered him to stop?
>
> **Faithful**: I did not know at first. But as he passed by, I noticed the holes in his hands and in his side. I concluded that he was our Lord. So I went up the Hill.
>
> **Christian**: The man who attacked you was Moses. He spares none. He does not know how to show mercy to transgressors of the Law" (Nelson's Royal Classics, Bunyan, John, 1999, p. 62).

Although influential, this characterization is not entirely accurate. As we saw earlier in this chapter, God had mercy on a large portion of the Israelites: Instead of destroying hundreds of thousands, he destroyed only 3,000. Praise the Lord, neither are we as Christians completely battered down by the law. Our provision is the comfort and mercy of the Spirit!

GOD PROVIDES FOR THOSE WHO ARE FAR OFF

It is fairly easy for non-Jewish, American Christians to see that Gentiles were included in God's plan of salvation, but for Peter and the other disciples, this was not immediately obvious. After all, Gentiles worshipped idols, not the God of Israel. And the law the Jewish people grew up with prevented any association with Gentiles. Jews could not go into Gentile houses, could not eat Gentile food, and could not marry Gentiles. The Gentiles persecuted Jews. Adding insult to injury, the Jewish people at that time were even forced to live under the Gentile rulers of Rome.

Since the Feast of Weeks was a Jewish feast, it would seem reasonable that only Jews were present at the time of the giving of the Spirit at this feast. The newly begun church, made up of those first 3,000 plus those they were adding day by day, was most likely completely Jewish. It is apparently some time before the disciples realize salvation through the Messiah is not meant for the Jews alone. After all, Gentiles were not awaiting a Messiah. What use would it have been to tell them about Him? In Acts 10, however, Peter realizes with the conversion of Cornelius that the Gentiles have also been included.

Read Peter's remarks in Acts 10:34-35, 45-48.

1. What did Peter do for the Gentiles who received the Holy Spirit (Acts 10:47)?

____

____

____

Read Acts 11:16-18.

2. How did Peter defend this action to the apostles?

____

____

3. What did God grant "to the Gentiles also" in Acts 11:18?

____

____

Currently, the traditional readings for Shavuot still emphasize Deuteronomy 29:12-15.

4. According to these verses, with whom was God making the covenant (v. 15)?

____

____

Read Acts 2:39 and Ephesians 2:11-22.

5. Who were the people God had in mind when he talked about those who were "far off"?

____

6. From Ephesians 2:11-22, list some of the advantages of being included.

____

____

Did you notice that we, the Gentiles, are the ones who are "far off" in Deuteronomy 29? It is exciting to see ourselves in the Old Testament. Just like Ruth, God provided for us even before we existed.

7. Who are "both groups" mentioned in Ephesians 2:14?

____

8. How are they reconciled (v. 16)?

___

9. At this point, do you have any insight as to the meaning of the two leavened loaves that we read about in the first section of this chapter?

___

In Old Testament times, the two leavened loaves are held up before the altar on the Feast of Weeks. God sees that neither loaf is acceptable. They are leavened. Sinful. The Jews are unable to keep the law, and animal sacrifice is needed to atone for sin. Gentiles are unacceptable because they do not even know God. They are worshiping man-made idols. But in God's mind, from ancient times, He sees you and me and a time when these feasts won't need to be celebrated this way anymore. Jesus will die as our Passover Lamb. He will be buried as our Leaven, and He will rise from the dead as the First Fruits. With the very Spirit of God indwelling both Jew and Gentile at the Feast of Weeks, finally both sinful loaves are acceptable before God. Not on our own merits, but on the righteous nature of our sinless Passover Lamb: one provision, one perfect sacrifice, even for those who were far off. We are all now acceptable to God.

The inclusion of the Gentiles helps to explain the two leavened loaves of bread that were required as the first offering before the Lord on Pentecost. The first three feasts (Passover, Unleavened Bread and First Fruits) collectively focus on purging leaven to celebrate the feast. Purging the leaven was symbolic of purging sin from their lives. We saw this as pointing toward the sinless nature of Christ. The Feast of Weeks, however, is a feast containing leaven. It focuses on sinful man and his inability to keep the covenant God has made with him. There are really only two types of people as far as God is concerned: Jew and Gentile. We can see these two leavened loaves representing these two groups of people: both with sin, both acceptable by God only through the new covenant of grace. Gentiles, therefore, have been "grafted in," according to Paul in Romans 11:17. But while the early church was almost fully Jewish, the church today is almost fully Gentile. With all the symbolism in the feasts that Jews still keep to this day, one has to wonder why, sadly, the Jewish people, in general, do not recognize Jesus as the Messiah. We will consider this question in the next section.

God provides grace

The original Church was nearly all Jewish. The big question dealt with in the book of Galatians is, "Can a Gentile be saved? And if so, do they need to keep the entire law and be circumcised?" Today, the situation is reversed. The church is almost all Gentile. We ask, "Can a Jew be saved?"

Read Romans 11:6-24.

1. There are several reasons listed why the Jews corporately have not embraced Jesus as their Messiah. List the ones you find in the following verses:

Rom. 11:8

____

Rom. 11:9

____

Rom. 11:10

____

Rom. 11:11

____

Rom. 11:12

____

Rom. 11:15

____

Rom. 11:19

____

2. In Romans 11:16-24, who are the wild olive branches?

____

3. Who are the natural branches?

____

4. What should our attitude be toward the natural branches?

____

____

5. Is there hope for salvation for the Jews (include verse)?

____

Romans 1:16-17 says, "For I am not ashamed of the gospel, for it is the power of God for salvation to everyone who believes, to the Jew first and also to the Greek. For in it the righteousness of God is revealed from faith to faith; as it is written, "But the righteous man shall live by faith."

Consider Psalm 122:6-9.

6. How could you pray for the Jews and for the nation of Israel?

____

____

In Romans 11, we have looked at some scripture references offering some reasons why the Jews "don't get it." Probably the biggest reason that the Jewish people today have a hard time seeing Jesus as their Messiah is due to the "Christian" church. Many churches teach a concept called "replacement theology." This doctrine teaches that God rejected the Jews when they rejected Jesus and crucified him, that the Church has now inherited all of the promises that were originally given to the Jews, that the Church has replaced Israel as God's chosen people, and that since God has no more use for the Jews, the Church has no need for them either. With this mindset, the "Christian" church has justified innumerable acts of violence against the Jews. This is true of the Protestant and Catholic churches alike. With so many of their ancestors and relatives killed in the name of Christ, it is no wonder that the name of Jesus is considered a curse word in many Jewish homes. What a tragedy that a misinterpretation of scripture could cause so much more than a mere stumbling block, but rather a huge chasm, in reaching modern Jewish people for Christ!

We believe that the proper interpretation of scripture is that the Church does not replace Israel in its national covenant relationship with God. Rather than replacing Israel as God's chosen people, the Church is God's method for spreading the gospel in this age. We are "grafted in," as the above passage in Romans 11 says. In fact, only as recently as the 1990s, a "grafted in" symbol was found on Mount Zion and brought to the world's attention. It is believed to have been used by early Messianic Jewish believers and is made up of an intertwined menorah, a Star of David, and a fish symbol. On some artifacts, the fish's eye is a tiny cross (Schmalz, 1999).

7. Read 2 Corinthians 3. Using these verses and what we have learned this week, complete the following:

Read Hebrews 12:18-29.

Old Covenant Pentecost	New Covenant Pentecost
Fiftieth Day	Fiftieth Day
Commandments written on ____________________	Commandments written on hearts and minds
3,000 people killed	__________ people saved
Letter of the law __________	Spirit gives __________
Glory on the face of ____________________	Glory found in Jesus
Glory fades	Glory ______________
	Veil removed in Christ
Mt. Sinai	Mt. Zion
Two leavened loaves	

8. Using these verses, list any differences you notice between the old covenant of the law and the new covenant of grace.

Law	**Grace**
____________________	____________________
____________________	____________________
____________________	____________________
____________________	____________________
____________________	____________________
____________________	____________________

____________________ ____________________

____________________ ____________________

As we have studied the Feast of Weeks, or Pentecost, we have seen that the Holy Spirit fulfills this feast. He brings us peace and comfort. He nudges our hearts to praise our God who delivers us from bondage. He is seen and heard as wind and fire, and as such, He blows away the useless chaff in our lives and purifies our hearts so that "we receive a kingdom which cannot be shaken" (Hebrews 12:28).

Because of the new covenant of grace, we are freed from the consequences of breaking the laws of the Torah, and in spite of our sin and shortcomings, we have friendship with God. He kept the old covenant and provided the perfect sacrifice; He then provided a new covenant, even though we were ignorant that we needed it. He provided the Spirit, a Comforter for our every need. Hallelujah, what a Savior! And yet, there are three feasts left to observe. What more could He possibly have for us?

CHAPTER SEVEN

FEAST OF TRUMPETS (Rosh Hashanah)

— *A Lesson in Victory*

The sound was chilling, haunting in its reverberations throughout the room, piercing in its reach to our very soul, urging us to act, to stand, to applaud, to … do something! But in our state of awe, we sat. We had never heard a sound like it. A lady held two long, spiraled, ram's horns to her mouth and simultaneously coaxed two different sounds out of each horn. The blasts were a call to attention, yet projected a comforting melody. One hundred sounds echoed off the walls before an intense silence rested on the small gathering. It was Rosh Hashanah (Feast of Trumpets), and we were privileged to be observing it with a group of Messianic Jewish believers. As we listened, captivated by these beautiful sounds, we were reminded of our experience several years before at the base of the southern wall surrounding the Temple Mount in Jerusalem.

We were touring the Old City and stood among the then-recent archaeological finds, including the top corner of the original temple wall now toppled and lying in the newly excavated first-century street below. The original piece of stone containing a Hebrew inscription had been carefully removed and taken to an Israeli museum, but a reproduction had been re-cast and attached back to the top of the stone block. It read, "To the place of the trumpeting" (Negev & Gibson, 2001). Could this really be the stone where a priest blew a trumpet to begin the Feast of Trumpets during the time of Jesus? We surmised that perhaps Satan led Jesus to this very place, high at the corner of the wall where trumpet blasts announced important proclamations, to tempt Jesus to throw Himself off (Matthew 4:5-6). We could imagine walking among throngs of people in the city of that time period when an explosion of sound from the ram's horn might bring all to a standstill and compel each person to listen at attention. At His second coming, might Jesus return to this actual place at the sound of the shofar and call all believers to Him?

In the quiet moments, as the last sound from the shofar lingered in the room, we couldn't help but think of the words to a familiar hymn, "*The trump shall resound, and the Lord shall descend, even so, it is well with my soul …*" (Horatio G. Spafford, 1873).

God blows his own shofar

God has a plan for Israel. He will not forget His people. In the previous chapter, we briefly discussed "Replacement Theology," the idea that the Jewish people have been replaced by the church. In contrast, our view is that the church has not replaced Israel, but has been grafted in to the promises and grace extended to them. Let's look at a couple of biblical passages that seem to validate the belief that the Jewish people are still God's chosen people and that they have not been "un-chosen." In fact, we believe God is using Israel as His prophetic time clock. Watching God's faithfulness to Israel as His prophecy is fulfilled encourages us in our faith. He is not just some god from long ago in fantastical stories of drama and intrigue. We are reminded that God is still at work in our world today, and He is still fulfilling His promises both to the nation of Israel and to us as believers in Him.

Jeremiah 31:35-37 reads,

> *"Thus says the LORD, Who gives the sun for light by day, and the fixed order of the moon and the stars for light by night, Who stirs up the sea so that its waves roar; The LORD of hosts is His name: 'If this fixed order departs from before Me,' declares the LORD, 'Then the offspring of Israel also shall cease from being a nation before Me forever.' Thus says the LORD, 'If the heavens above can be measured, and the foundations of the earth searched out below, then I will also cast off all the offspring of Israel for all that they have done,' declares the LORD."*

Ezekiel 16:60-63 states,

> *"Nevertheless, I will remember My covenant with you in the days of your youth, and I will establish an everlasting covenant with you. Then you will remember your ways and be ashamed when you receive your sisters, both your older and your younger; and I will give them to you as daughters, but not because of your covenant. Thus I will establish My covenant with you, and you shall know that I am the LORD, in order that you may remember and be ashamed, and never open your mouth anymore because of your humiliation, when I have forgiven you for all that you have done,' the Lord GOD declares."*

Even if they do not corporately acknowledge the Messiah at this time, scripture promises that a remnant of Israel will be saved in the latter days. The feasts we are about to study demonstrate this plan God still has for His beloved nation of Israel, the blood descendants of Abraham, Isaac, and Jacob.

In our study so far, while we have seen how the first four feasts have been literally fulfilled by Christ and by the Holy Spirit, the remaining three feasts have not yet had their ultimate fulfillment. After the Feast of Weeks, there is a four-month waiting period until the next set of feasts. Most theologians agree that this represents the harvest period or the church age that we are in now. God is waiting for the full "harvest" of believers to come in before continuing with the fulfillment of His feasts (Romans 11:25-32).
Read John 4:34-39.

1. How long did the disciples say it was until the harvest (v. 35)?

____

2. When did Christ say the harvest was (v. 35)?

____

3. In verse 37, Jesus says, "One sows, and another reaps." What do you think they are sowing and reaping?

____

Like the first three feasts, the last three (Trumpets, Day of Atonement, and Tabernacles) come in fairly rapid succession in the Jewish yearly calendar. However, their fulfillment in the new covenant is yet to come.

Read Leviticus 23:23-25 and Numbers 29:1-6.

4. What were the Israelites supposed to do on the first day of the seventh month?

____

____

During the First Temple Period, this feast was called the Feast of Trumpets (Yom Truah or Day of Sounding) because it was a "reminder by blowing trumpets" and a "day for blowing trumpets." While it is still referred to by this title today, it is also called Rosh Hashanah (Hebrew for "head of the year"). It is celebrated as the Jewish New Year even though it is celebrated in their seventh month. "*Shanah*" means year, and "*tov*" means good. So, the greeting for this day is "*Shanah tovah,*" or "Have a good year." Or, "*Leshanah tovah tikatevu*" which means, "May God write you in the Book of Life for a good year." We will talk more about the current Jewish traditions concerning Rosh Hashanah throughout this chapter. We can learn quite a bit about this feast by learning more about the trumpet (also called the *shofar*, the Hebrew word for ram's horn). The shofar is rich in history and is discussed in both the Old and New Testaments. For background information, we are going to look at this history in the Old and New Testament scripture and its significance to us and to Israel. As you study, keep in mind that these festivals are "a mere shadow of what is to come; but the substance belongs to Christ" (Colossians 2:17).

Read Genesis 22:1-18. (This is the primary synagogue reading for Rosh Hashanah.)

5. What did God ask Abraham to do (v. 2)?

____

____

6. Where was Abraham supposed to go to do this (v. 2)?

____

7. What is Abraham's response to Isaac in verse eight?

____

____

8. In verse 13, how did God provide the offering for Abraham to use in Isaac's place?

____

The rabbis teach that this is the first use of horns to save God's chosen people. This took place on Mount Moriah, which today is the location of the Temple Mount in Jerusalem.

9. What did Abraham name the place?

____

10. Take a moment to list some things and thank God for what He has provided for you in the past week.

____

____

____

____

11. Who was the Lamb God provided for our salvation?

____

12. Because Abraham "obeyed My voice," who would be blessed (v. 18)?

____

Read Galatians 3:6-9.

13. Who was God talking about when He told Abraham, "All the nations shall be blessed in you" (v. 8)?

____

14. How are they justified?

____

According to Jewish tradition, Rosh Hashanah was the day when Abraham showed his obedience to God by being willing to sacrifice his son Isaac. God provided a ram for Abraham to sacrifice in place of Isaac. The ram was caught by its horn in the thicket.

Let's look at Genesis 22:13 again:

> *"Then Abraham raised his eyes and looked, and behold, behind him a ram caught in the thicket by his horns; and*

> *Abraham went and took the ram, and offered him up for a burnt offering in the place of his son."*

In verse 23 where it says "behind him," the Hebrew word is *achar*, which means "afterward" or "in the future" (Lockman Foundation, 1998, p. 1359). The Jews have a saying, "Here now, but not yet." Hebrew writings see the ram as representing the Messiah, and the thicket stands for the sins of the people. When Abraham saw the ram caught in the thicket, he was really looking forward and seeing Yeshua (Jesus) being sacrificed for the sins of the people. So from the beginning, when a ram's horn saved Isaac, the shofar has become synonymous with deliverance throughout Israel's history.

This information causes John 8:56 to make more sense:

> *"Your father Abraham rejoiced to see My day, and he saw it and was glad.' The Jews therefore said to Him, 'You are not yet fifty years old, and have You seen Abraham?' Jesus said to them, 'Truly, truly, I say to you, before Abraham was born, I am.' Therefore they picked up stones to throw at Him; but Jesus hid Himself, and went out of the temple."*

Indeed, God Himself provided a sacrifice. From Abraham's time on, Jesus was "here now, not yet," the fulfillment of God's demand for a perfect sacrifice. Then in God's timing, thousands of years after Abraham, Jesus was sacrificed for the Jews as well as the Gentiles. By faith in the Lamb that God provided, Jews and Gentiles alike can now be justified.

As you go through your day today, remember how the God of history is accomplishing His will in every era, including this one. We often think how God designed us perfectly for this time in history. For Carl, he gets to do work that physicians 50 years ago only dreamed of. And for Dallas, life without a microwave or running water would be disastrous; she can barely cook as it is! Seriously, though, just as Jesus was rejected by some in his day, his followers, too, can expect to face opposition, even in our current age of prosperity and convenience. Like Jesus, we can trust God in the midst of trial, darkness, and suffering. We find comfort in 1 Peter 1:7, where it tells us that our trials are necessary: "That the proof of your faith, being more precious than gold which is perishable, even though tested by fire, may be found to result in praise and glory and honor at the revelation of Jesus Christ." The great news is that eventually, when the shofar sounds, we will be delivered and our Savior will appear!

OLD TESTAMENT MEN BLOW THE SHOFAR

Read Joshua 6:1-20. (What a great story! If you care to read the entire account, finish the chapter reading through verse 27. If you care to confirm the fulfillment of the prophecy in verse 26, read 1 Kings 16:34.)

1. From verse one, what do you think the people of Jericho thought of the Israelites?

____

2. What did God tell the Israelites to do in order to conquer Jericho?

____

It's interesting to note here that these are specific details and instructions for conquering this particular city. The Israelites did not use this method for conquering every city. They learned to trust in God and to wait for His precise commands. They were not dependent on a specific method that worked to deliver them; they waited for new instructions for each new battle. For each situation, they were reliant on the mighty power and wisdom of God, not a fixed formula, for victory.

3. What were the seven priests supposed to carry before the ark (v. 4)?

____

____

4. When did the people begin shouting in verse 20, and what happened after they did?

____

5. Where did the people go after the walls fell down (v. 20)?

____

____

We have mentioned before that the name "Jesus" is not a true translation of the Hebrew word *Yeshua*. The name Jesus comes from a Greek transliteration of the name Yeshua. A transliteration roughly means what the word sounds like in one language when it is written in another. A better English translation for Yeshua is Joshua. Knowing this, we can better appreciate the picture of Joshua being a type (or foreshadowing) of the Messiah. Just as he led his people up into the promised land, we are trusting Jesus to do the same thing. He leads His people (Christ-followers, all those who belong to Him) up into the promised land (Heaven) to live eternally with Him.

Read 1 Thessalonians 4:16-17.

6. Where will we, as believers in Christ, go when we hear the trumpet of God?

____

____

Read Judges 7:1-25.

7. Why did God only want "a few good men" for Gideon to take into battle (v. 2)?

____

8. Why do you think God chose the ones who brought their hand to their mouth to drink rather than the ones who knelt down to drink? (Just a thought question; there is no right or wrong answer.)

____

9. What characteristic of God do you see displayed in verses 9 through 11?

____

____

10. What did Gideon give each man (v. 16)?

____

11. Besides hearing the trumpets, what did the Midianites see (v. 20)?

____

____

Maybe soldiers who bring their hands to their mouths to drink are in a position to always be watching. If we are always watching for direction from the Lord, we can be victorious in whatever battle we encounter. He leads us with encouragement and compassion. He guards us from fear and doubt. And if we are exclusively dependent on Him, we cannot become boastful or proud. During the time of Gideon, it is thought that the blowing of the trumpet in battle was a summons for a battalion of men (about 400). Just imagine how many men the Midianites thought the Israelites had ready to fight!

The word for pitchers, in this verse, implies that the containers were made from earthenware or that they were earthen vessels. In other words, they were not clear or transparent. When the pitchers were crushed, there would have been instant light from many different areas. What an impact we could have if we would allow our earthly vessels to be crushed so that God's light inside us could shine forth with power! Can you imagine the effect in the spiritual realm when we join together, united as believers in Jesus and surrender our fleshly desires to God? What a great, shining light that must be!

12. What ways could you let God's light shine forth in you today?

____

____

13. What happened when the Israelites blew the 300 trumpets (v. 22)?

____

____

14. After Gideon's initial stand against Midian, who else came to help (vv. 23-24)?

____

15. Relate a time when you have taken the first step in faith and then God has sent "help."

____

____

____

____

MODERN DAY MEN BLOW THE SHOFAR

In the previous section, we learned about the part the trumpet played in times of war for the Israelites. In this section, we're going to take a small detour from the trumpet to look a little deeper into the history of Israel's wars and at God's faithfulness to deliver His chosen people. We've already seen how Joshua was victorious at the city of Jericho and how Gideon was triumphant over the Midianites. After Gideon won that battle, he pursued the kings of Midian: Zebah and Zalmunna.

Let's read this story in Judges 8:18-24.

1. What did Gideon take from Zebah and Zalmunna after he killed them (v. 21)?

____

2. From what descendants were Gideon's enemies (v. 24)?

____

To understand more about this particular conflict and the one that still rages in the Middle East today, it's helpful to have a little more background on Ishmael. Ishmael was born to Abram and Hagar (Sarai's Egyptian maid, see Genesis 16:1). After Ishmael was born, God changed Abram's and Sarai's names to Abraham and Sarah. Later, Isaac (Ishmael's half brother) was born to Abraham and Sarah. Isaac had Jacob, whose name was later changed to Israel. The Jews of today are descendants of Israel, and the Arabs are descendants of Ishmael.

Read Genesis 16:7-12.

3. What do you learn about the descendants of Ishmael from verse 10?

____

4. What will Ishmael be like (v. 12)?

____

____

____

____

5. Where will Ishmael's descendants live (v. 12)?

____

6. Who are Ishmael's "brothers"?

____

Instead of Isaac, the Arabs believe that it was Ishmael who was almost sacrificed on the altar by Abraham on Mount Moriah (Genesis 22:1-2). As for God's promise that Ishmael would have too many descendants to count, consider the current populations in the Middle East. There are 21 Arab nations with a combined population of approximately 300 million people. There is one Jewish state (Israel) with a population of about 7.6 million; about 75 percent who are Jews (Eglesh, 2010). The Jewish population worldwide, as of 2010, is just over 13 million

(DellaPergola, 2010). That's a worldwide Arab to Jewish population ratio of approximately 23:1.

The majority of Arab lands today (Syria, Jordan, Iran, Iraq, Saudi Arabia, Kuwait, Yemen, Oman, and others) are to the east of Israel, just as Genesis 16:12 says. And, of course, the Arabs and Israelis are still in conflict with one another. We see the "wild donkey of a man," that Genesis 16:12 speaks of, in the current political climate of Arab nations, including Arab against Arab in the Gulf War example of Iraq

invading Kuwait (January 1991). Also, the crescent symbol belonging to the Ishmaelites in the story of Gideon is still a symbol for the Arabs today in their religion of Islam.

Remember in our study of Gideon (Judges 7), that God was faithful to provide Gideon with victory over the enemy through surprise and cover of darkness, even though his men were outnumbered. Keeping what you learned about Gideon in mind, consider the following scenarios from Israel's War of Independence in May, 1948.

> "... Because it posed a potential threat to their lines of communication, the Egyptians first attacked the isolated Jewish village of Kfar Darom to the south between Khan Yunis and Gaza. Defended by 30 youths, and cut off for months, the village had already withstood a major attack by the Moslem Brotherhood, supported by artillery, on 10 May. The defenders had held their fire until the attackers reached the barbed-wire fence surrounding the village and then, with hand grenades and small arms, had fought back. When the defenders, orthodox Jews, had run out of hand grenades, they had even filled the small velvet bags in which they normally kept their phylacteries, worn during morning prayers, with TNT and thrown them as grenades at the attackers. Meanwhile, the Egyptian artillery supporting the attack had erred, so that instead of hitting the village its shells had landed among the attackers, causing chaos. The Brotherhood had broken, leaving some 70 dead and wounded on the battlefield. The morale-raising effect of this gallant defense on the isolated settlers throughout the Negev had been electrifying. However, an attempt to reinforce the settlement was intercepted by the Egyptians with the result that, while a small number of reinforcements did arrive, they brought with them comparatively large numbers of wounded to the already-overcrowded underground infirmary of the village. Then, on 15 May, the Egyptian

> Army attacked, led by a troop of tanks and two troops of armoured cars, but the infantry failed to keep up with the armour. As a result, the attack was broken: a number of armoured vehicles were disabled, and the infantry fell back with heavy losses. Thereafter, the Egyptians refrained from attempting to attack the village, but occupied all the high ground around it, to bring it under blockade. (Towards the end of the First Truce, when it was clear that fighting was about to be renewed, it became evident to the Israelis that there was no point in maintaining an isolated position so far behind the Egyptian lines, and the village was evacuated. The day after the stealthy evacuation of the village by the Israelis, the Egyptians opened up with a long artillery barrage, and then launched an attack … only to find Kfar Darom empty)" (Herzog, 1984, p. 70).

Below is a description of another battle in May 1948. Keep in mind that Tel Aviv was a pivotal stronghold for Israel in their War of Independence. Yadin was a top military leader for Israel at that time.

> "With a population of a quarter-million, Tel Aviv had burgeoned spectacularly into one of the most advanced and impressive cities of the Middle East; it was now more than three times larger than New Jerusalem, the former concentration of Jewish settlement. Its fall clearly would mean the end of the war for Israel. At this point, therefore, Yadin decided to risk a tactical offensive. On May 29 he ordered reinforcements from the Jerusalem Corridor to circle Naguib's positions at night and attack the Egyptians from the rear. With a troop strength barely half that of the invaders, the relief force nevertheless found darkness and surprise no less effective than had Sadeh and Wingate in the 1930s. The Egyptians were thrown into confusion by the unexpected descent upon their flank. Yadin shrewdly exploited their disarray by calling a press conference and

> announcing that the Egyptian supply lines had been cut by "overwhelming concentrations" of Israeli troops. The "news" was immediately dispatched over the international wire services, and eventually reached Cairo. As Yadin had hoped, the Egyptian high command accepted the story at face value and radioed Naguib to pull up short. The bewildered commander dutifully followed these instructions. Naguib's setback proved to be the turning point of the Egyptian invasion. Tel Aviv was never again in jeopardy" (Sachar, 1998, pp. 320-321).

7. What similarities do you see between Gideon's battle and these battles from 1948?

____

____

____

The elements of surprise and darkness served the Israelis well in both the battle with the Midianites and the 1948 battle for a new country to call their own. Also, both battles featured the enemy firing on themselves. Just as the shofar blasts announced the false message of numerous warriors that was received as truth by the Midianites' in an ancient generation, so, too, the twentieth-century Egyptians believed a bogus news announcement that turned the direction of the war for the Israelis.

In Israel's 1948 War of Independence, Israel became and was recognized a sovereign nation. However, the Israelis did not regain control of Jerusalem. It was not until the Six-Day War in 1967 that Israel reclaimed this city and the Temple Mount for the first time since its destruction in 70 A.D.

> "In June 1967, the haunting sound of the shofar again echoed on Jerusalem's Temple Mount after almost 1900 years. It was sounded by Chief Rabbi Shlomo Goren after Israeli soldiers restored Jewish sovereignty over East Jerusalem and reunited Israel's eternal capital (Howard & Rosenthal, 1997, p. 107)."

The Israelis, however, turned the control of the Temple Mount back over to the Arabs shortly after this victory. It remains in Arab control, but the Western Wall of the Temple Mount is accessible and in the control of the Jews. A prophecy in Daniel 9 suggests that there will be a temple again, so we can assume that one day the Jews will again control the Temple Mount.

8. How does God's intervention in Israel's struggles encourage you today?

____

____

____

It is absolutely fascinating to us that God is still the God of Israel. His word is still relevant and true. The validity of scripture is proven simply by the modern day political scene. Dallas' grandmother used to read her Bible wondering how some of it could be true. It spoke of a land called Israel, and yet there was no such land. In 1948, and shortly thereafter as it began to be clear that Israel would indeed survive as a nation, she shared with Dallas that she remembered thinking, *"God's word is true!"* For her, she had seen Isaiah 66:8 come to pass during her lifetime: "Who has ever heard of such a thing? Who has ever seen such things? Can a country be born in a day or a nation be brought forth in a moment? Yet no sooner is Zion in labor than she gives birth to her children" (NIV). Indeed, the nation of Israel was "born in a day … brought forth in a moment" on May 14, 1948, in a Tel Aviv museum as David Ben Gurion, the country's first prime minister, declared the independence of Israel.

LISTENING FOR THE SHOFAR OF THE SOUL

The Jewish author Ari Goldman, in his book *Being Jewish*, says, "… the sound of the shofar, the ram's horn … is a kind of spiritual alarm clock for the soul" (Goldman, 2000, p. 108). While we don't have a literal fulfillment of these last three feasts, we can make some sound Biblical assumptions. Many prophecies in the Bible have a "pre-fillment" before the fulfillment. These last three feasts may have that "pre-fillment" in the life of a believer in Jesus. Realizing God is calling us to Himself is a type of shofar our soul hears. However, as we have seen the first four feasts literally fulfilled, it would follow that these last three will be literally fulfilled also. Since this is prophecy, there are many possible ways it could be fulfilled. The three major possibilities are: 1) Rapture of believers, 2) Re-gathering of the Jews to Israel, 3) Jesus' final return to earth. We will look briefly at each of these in this section.

The first consideration is that the Feast of Trumpets may be fulfilled by the rapture. The word "rapture" literally means "caught up." We read in 1 Thessalonians 4 that "we who are alive and remain shall be caught up" at the sound of the trumpet of God. We looked at these verses in Thessalonians in our study on Passover. We saw how Jesus played the role of the Bridegroom and called Christian believers His bride. We learned about the Jewish wedding customs, and how the bridegroom traditionally came for his bride like a thief in the night. It is possible to view the rapture as Jesus returning for His bride.

Read 1 Corinthians 15:49-52.

1. When will we all be changed?

____

2. How fast will we be changed?

____

3. What do you think that it means by "we shall not all sleep, but we shall all be changed"?

____

____

Just as the perishable cannot inherit the imperishable, it follows that we will be changed. Some people will still be alive at the rapture and so will not "sleep," but we will all be changed in that we will have glorified bodies.

The most controversial aspect of the rapture is its timing. There are three main ideas for when the rapture will occur. These all revolve around the seven-year period of the tribulation. The three possibilities are that the rapture will occur either at the beginning of the tribulation, the middle, or the end. There is simply not enough detail about this particular event in scripture to make an exact prediction. We recognize and respect the differing opinions on this issue of the timing of the rapture. To go into a detailed review of each of these viewpoints, however, is beyond the scope of this study. One aspect of Christ's return, however, that the Bible clearly discusses, is imminence: The warning in scripture is that the Lord may return at any moment.

Read Matthew 24:36-44.

4. Who knows when the Son of Man will come (v. 36)?

___

5. What will the coming of the Son of Man be like?

___

6. How are we to be waiting?

___

Since the Bible tells us that the rapture could occur at any moment and that no one will know when it is going to happen, it seems likely that it will take place sometime before the tribulation. If the rapture happened during the middle of the tribulation, we would be able to calculate that timing (once the tribulation began). This would also be true if it happened at the end of the tribulation.

The biggest argument against the rapture being the fulfillment of the Feast of Trumpets is that we would know each year what day to be looking for it to occur. This, by the way, is why "date setters" who predict the end of the world usually pick a date in the fall. They understand that the next feast yet to be fulfilled is the Feast of Trumpets.

Just as the days of Noah witnessed lewd and vulgar living, our current society is also observing similar practices. Jesus told us that the Father knows the time, and we should be waiting expectantly. How exciting it will be to hear that trumpet call us to Jesus - no more tears, no more injustice, no more wars!

Another major possibility for the fulfillment of the Feast of Trumpets is the re-gathering of the Jews to Israel. In 70 A.D., the Romans under Titus destroyed the temple, and the Jews were once again dispersed throughout the world. But long before they were dispersed, the Bible prophesied the eventual re-gathering of the Jews to Israel.

Read Ezekiel 37:1-14.

7. What was covering the ground of the valley where Ezekiel walked?

____

8. In verse four, what was Ezekiel commanded to do?

____

9. What happened as Ezekiel prophesied?

____

____

10. In verse 11, who do the bones represent?

____

11. Where will God bring them (v. 11)?

____

It is important to note here that the name of the land is given. It is called Israel: not Zion, not Holy Land, not Judah, but Israel. In the early days of Zionism, it was not clear that Israel would be the land for the Jews. Britain offered to make them a nation in Africa. The early leaders accepted this proposal because "at least they would have a nation." But later, the delegates at the Zionist's congress voted that proposal down. The majority of the delegates were swayed by the idea that only the land of Israel could be a national homeland that would inspire Jews to migrate from the nations and lands where they had become dispersed.

This re-gathering to Israel is already happening. In 1900, there were 40,000 Jews in the land that was to become known as Israel. In 1948, with the birth of the nation of Israel, there were 500,000. As we mentioned earlier, as of 2010, about 5.6 million of Israel's 7.6 million people are Jewish (DellaPergola, 2010).

Scholars who take the viewpoint of a re-gathering of Jews fulfilling the Feast of Trumpets believe that in the future, there will be a major event that brings all of the Jews to Israel. Of course, the Holocaust certainly instigated a population migration, but the rapture could be another event that facilitates a massive return of Jews to Israel. Believers would go to be with the Bridegroom, leaving the Jews no sympathetic ally. Jews may have no other place to go that is not hostile, except to Israel.

A third option for the fulfillment of this feast is the Second Coming of Jesus on the Feast of Trumpets. This could occur, not at the rapture, but at the time when Jesus sets foot on the Mount of Olives. Zechariah 14: 4 says, "And in that day His feet will stand on the Mount of Olives, which is in front of Jerusalem on the east …."

Read Matthew 24:29-31.

12. How will He send forth His angels?

___

13. What will the angels do?

___

(We will take a more in-depth look at this idea of the Second Coming in our study on the Feast of Tabernacles.)

No matter how the Feast of Trumpets is literally fulfilled, the bottom line is that we know the signal: It is the sound of the shofar that will call believers to their God.

14. How do you know you will be among the ones "caught up"?

____

____

1 John 5:11-13 tells us that we can know that we have eternal life, "And the witness is this, that God has given us eternal life, and this life is in His Son. He who has the Son has the life; he who does not have the Son of God does not have the life. These things I have written to you who believe in the name of the Son of God, in order that you may know that you have eternal life."

RETURNING TO THE SOUND OF GOD'S SHOFAR

Read Isaiah 27:12-13 with Isaiah 19:24-25

1. What will happen to the sons of Israel?

____

____

2. How will they be gathered?

____

Read Exodus 19:12-19.

3. Where were the people supposed to go (v. 13)?

____

4. When were they supposed to go (v. 13)?

____

5. What happened to the people when they heard the trumpet (v. 16)?

____

> *"Then the LORD will appear over them, and His arrow will go forth like lightning; and the Lord GOD will blow the trumpet, and will march in the storm winds of the south. The LORD of hosts will defend them. And they will devour, and trample on the sling stones; and they will drink, and be boisterous as with wine; and they will be filled like a sacrificial basin, drenched like the corners of the altar. And the LORD their God will save them in that day as the flock of His people; for they are as the stones of a crown, sparkling in His land"* (Zechariah 9:14-16).

In this section, we will look at some of the traditional ways that Jews celebrate the Feast of Trumpets. Even though God told the Israelites in Leviticus 23 to celebrate Passover as the beginning of their year, where the first month is specified as Aviv (or Nissan), Jews probably began to observe the Feast of Trumpets as the beginning of the year for a couple of reasons. First, the Feast of Trumpets works as the head of their year because it begins the waiting for the Day of Atonement. Everyone is hoping to be written in the Book of Life for another year. And as stated earlier, the common name for this feast is Rosh Hashanah, which means "head of the year." When the Israelites returned from Babylonian captivity, they had been influenced in many ways, and they changed most of the names of the months to Babylonian names. During this Second Temple Period, the seventh month was changed to be the first month. Today in Judaism, this calendar persists.

This Jewish New Year celebration is not a time of partying, but a time of repentance. Rosh Hashanah begins a period called *Teshuvah*, which is Hebrew for "returning to God." This period is also called the Ten Days of Awe. This is a time of reconciliation - a time to ask forgiveness from those you have hurt during the past year. It is also a time of charity.

From the First Temple Period, when God called this feast *Yom Truah*, the Feast of Trumpets, up through current Rosh Hashana celebrations, it has been commanded that everyone should hear the shofar on Rosh Hashanah. To ensure that everyone has the opportunity to hear the trumpet blast, rabbis visit hospitals and shut-ins. The sound of the shofar reminds Jews that sacrifice is sometimes necessary. They also feel that it asks God, for Abraham's sake, to forgive their sins. During the course of this feast, Jewish people will hear 100 blasts of the shofar. It is thought that the blasts will confuse Satan while he is trying to accuse Israel.

In the Temple Period, when the shofar was blown from the temple, no matter what the Jew was doing, all harvesting was to stop, and he was to go to the temple. If a Jew and Gentile were in the fields working, the Gentile would continue working. But a Jewish man would go straight to the temple at the sound of the shofar. This was a time of gathering people to Jerusalem.

The traditional foods eaten during this time include apples that are dipped in honey. Jews are hopeful that this will bring them a sweet New Year. Challah is prepared in a round loaf rather than the traditional shape. This shape is like the crown of a mighty ruler, and therefore reminds them of God's presence. It also symbolizes the never-ending cycle of life. Jews also eat a fish head during this holiday in hopes that they will be the "head" in the New Year and not the "tail."

Read Micah 7:18-19.

6. What does God promise in this passage?

____

7. Where will God "cast their sins"?

____

One tradition associated with Rosh Hashanah is Tashlich, which means "to cast off." This tradition is based on the above passage from Micah. Jews walk to the edge of a stream, a lake, or the ocean (sometimes with breadcrumbs in their pockets as a symbol of sin). Then they cast the crumbs on the water, thus, symbolically casting their sins away.

There is a story of one elderly Jew who never participated in this custom. He relates that as a child, he was watching from afar as nicely dressed adults approached the beach to cast their sins into the sparkling water before them.

> "Suddenly the winds changed and a great wave came up on shore, splashing them all — the men, the women, and the children. A great cry rose up from the crowd, and they ran, in wet shoes, to higher ground. It was then that I realized that God does not want our sins (Goldman, 2000, p. 115)."

While God may not want our sins, He is certainly faithful to forgive our sins and to tread our iniquities underfoot as mentioned in the passage we read in Micah above. This is declared in one of the traditional readings for the Tashlich ceremony.

Read Psalm 130.

8. If God kept a record of our sins, what would be our chance for redemption (v. 3)?

____

____

9. What can be found in the Lord (v. 7)?

____

10. Spend some time meditating on Psalm 130. Cast any sin that comes to your mind on Him. Praise Him that you are totally forgiven the moment you accept Christ's sacrifice.

As we discussed earlier, one of the fulfillments of the Feast of Trumpets may be when Jesus returns at the Second Coming. If this is the case, it is fascinating to consider some of the specific details of the service that take place in the synagogue during this feast. Blu Greenberg, in her book, *How to Run a Traditional Jewish Household*, describes the service beginning early with a calling out loudly: "HA'MELECH — THE KING, as if to announce the entry of the King, seated on His throne in the heavenly court .... We clap our right hand over our left breast as a sign of remorse and guilt and say, 'Our Father, we have sinned before You.' Then prayers are offered for God's saving grace" (Greenberg, 1983, p. 325).

What rich traditions that are related to the Jewish feasts! Before Christ was ever born, God's grace was described in scripture as "casting our sins into the deepest seas," and the feasts foreshadowed the coming of Jesus the Savior who would be the incarnation of God's loving kindness.

If this feast is fulfilled at the Second Coming of Christ, it is amazing to think that at the very time Jesus returns to the Mount of Olives, the Jewish people in their synagogues around the world will be sounding the shofar, praying for forgiveness and grace, calling out loudly, "HA'MELECH — THE KING!" What a beautiful picture of exactly how we should be waiting for our King. Sound the trumpet; come quickly, Lord Jesus!

CHAPTER EIGHT

DAY OF ATONEMENT (Yom Kippur)

— *A Lesson on the Best*

On one New Year's Eve in Aguas Callientes, fear and frustration worked into our thoughts as we were lying wide awake in our tiny, Peruvian hotel room. Sleep was hopeless. Music blasted from a dance bar below us, random fireworks (at least that's what we hoped they were) echoed through the streets, drunken people staggered along the sidewalks, and a raging river roared right outside our window. By 4 a.m., we decided we might as well get up and be the first ones in line at the bus stop. Our three older children, all teenagers, and we were hoping to obtain five passes out of only 400 given out daily for the opportunity to climb Huayna Pichu, the mountain that towers above the ruins of Machu Pichu.

Boarding the bus and arriving at the ruins, our sleepless night paid off as we raced to the far end of Machu Pichu, scarcely taking in any of the sights, and found ourselves third in line for the climb. Some young men were in line in front of us. We could hear them bragging to one another about their physical fitness and how quickly they thought they could make it to the top. Each one of our family had recently run a half-marathon, and without even speaking it to one another, we were all thinking the same thing, "We can take 'em!"

The precautions for hiking conditions in a tourist area in Peru are not quite as conservative as in America. In fact, the trail is so narrow in some places that one wrong step could send you falling to your death thousands of feet below. There are no guard rails protecting the edge, no caution signs. Occasionally, on a particularly treacherous stretch, there might be a short length of steel cable drilled into the mountain to use as a handrail, or an ancient-looking wooden ladder to help you progress down a steep cliff. Our son, Connor, joked that probably the only reason a ladder or cable was there is that someone had already died at that spot. Hiking there is definitely at your own risk. The only safeguard is upon entering the trail. You must log in your passport number and sign your name. We were hopeful that this meant some sort of rescue might be launched at the end of the day if we hadn't signed back out. Our family's often quoted comment during the climb was, "You could die here!"

We signed in our passport numbers as quickly as possible and began jogging up the trail. At close to 9,000 feet above sea level, climbing Huayna Pichu was like running a marathon while breathing through a straw. Nevertheless, our family triumphed as we were the first family atop the breathtaking mountain on the first day of the New Year. We were literally and emotionally on a mountaintop that reached above the clouds!

Hiking down proved to be more of a challenge than the trek up. En route down, we were forced to look down at our feet to avoid any missteps, and in so doing, there was no missing the view of the sheer drop at the edge of the trail. The trail was steep, wet, and narrow, and sharing the trail with the ascending hikers could easily prove perilous. We were hungry, thirsty, and exhausted from the climbing, the altitude, the danger, and the sleepless night. The thick clouds and drizzly weather mirrored our attitudes as our tempers became short with one another. As we rounded a bend, we noticed an outcropping in the rock wall and ducked underneath it. We found ourselves in a small, shallow cave with an enormous, empty nest in it. While we could still hear the rushing waters of the violent Urubamba River over 1,000 feet below us, it was quieter in the cave. This cleft in a rock felt like a sacred sanctuary.

We each found a spot to sit and rest for a moment, and God proceeded to pull back the cloudy curtain of His creation and put on a spectacular show for our tired family. A few sparsely scattered sunbeams began to penetrate the clouds. Then suddenly the fog and the clouds were gone, and the sun was bright and warm. Stretched before us were endless peaks of the most majestic, deep-green mountains we had ever seen. Carefully peering over the precipice, we could see the river crashing below us, offering up its violent chords in a cacophony of sound. The fatigue and danger of the climb was quickly forgotten as we rested in the cleft of the rock and witnessed the power and beauty of God's creation. Slowly, the fog and clouds rolled back into place and each of us felt, like Moses must have, as though we had just seen the glory of God pass by while we rested in the hollow of His hand (Exodus 33:22).

The peril of falling to our deaths had been very real throughout the day. The weariness of the climb threatened to overtake us, yet here we sat in a little hollowed-out space in a rock: safe, dry, at rest. We each enjoyed our own moments of worship as we listened to a song on Dallas' iPod and joined God's creation in bringing Him praise:

> *One day the trumpet will sound for His coming*
> *One day the skies with His glories will shine*
> *Wonderful day, my Beloved One's bringing*
> *Glorious Savior, this Jesus is mine.*
> *Living He loved me, dying He saved me.*
> *Buried He carried my sins far away.*
> *Rising He justified, freely forever*
> *One day He's coming*
> *Oh, Glorious Day!*
> *Oh, Glorious Day!* ("One Day," J.Wilbur Chapman, 1910)

One glorious day, Jesus will return for us, and as we learned from the Feast of Trumpets, we rejoice that our names are written in the Book of Life. Those unforgettable moments on Huayna Pichu evoked in us a sense of awe for God's majesty and filled us with a renewed, awestruck excitement for the day He will come for us — as we simply rested in the divinely created shelter we found in that mountainside.

The "Days of Awe" are the ten days between Rosh Hashanah (Feast of Trumpets) and Yom Kippur (The Day of Atonement) on the Jewish calendar. According to Jewish tradition, God will judge individuals during this time to determine whether they live or die. It is the last chance for repentance before God's judgment on the Day of Atonement. It is also a time of reconciliation and soul searching. The Jew fasts and prays that he will be found worthy to be written in the Book of Life for another year.

The best High Priest

Yom Kippur, or the Day of Atonement, is also known as Shabbat Shabbatan: the Sabbath of Sabbaths. We like to call it the "Best of Rest" because the word Sabbath means "rest." This is the rest of all rests. In fact, the Bible specifies only one day when fasting is required, and that is on Yom Kippur. In the days when Israel had a temple, atonement was based on the sacrifices offered by the High Priest. Today, without the ability to make those same animal sacrifices as prescribed at the temple, Jews believe the atonement is based on charity and good works that are emphasized during Yom Kippur.

Read Leviticus 23:26-32.

1. What purpose does this feast serve (v. 28)?

   ____

2. When was it supposed to be celebrated (v. 27)?

   ____

3. List each of the verses from this passage that refer to "humbling oneself" (NASB), "denying oneself" (NIV), or "afflicting one's soul" (KJV).

____

____

4. What do you think it means to "humble or deny yourself"?

____

5. What will happen to those who do not humble or deny themselves (v. 29)?

____

6. What will happen to anyone who does any work on this day (v. 30)?

____

7. Write out a definition for the word atonement. You may want to consult a dictionary, Bible dictionary, or look up cross-references in your Bible to formulate your definition.

____

Let's look at how Israel observed the Day of Atonement when Aaron was the high priest.

Read Leviticus 16.

8. From what were Aaron's clothes made (v. 4)?

____

9. What sacrifice was Aaron supposed to offer, and what was it for (v. 5)?

____

____

10. What were the two goats for and where was the one sent (vv.7-10, 15, 21)?

____

____

The one goat was sacrificed for the sins of the nation of Israel while the other goat was sent out into the wilderness with the guilt of that sin. In temple times, the goat was no longer set free to wander in the wilderness. It was taken outside of the city and pushed off a cliff.

We recognize in Jesus the sacrifice for our sin. In 2 Corinthians 5:21, scripture tells us that God "made Him who knew no sin to be sin on our behalf, that we might become the righteousness of God in Him." Jesus also fulfills the symbolism of the scapegoat by suffering outside of the city, as we read in Hebrews 13:12, "Therefore Jesus also, that He might sanctify the people through His own blood, suffered outside the gate." It is remarkable that God recognizes our need for forgiveness of sin, as well as our need for freedom from guilt.

11. What was the bull for (Lev. 16:11)?

____

12. What was Aaron supposed to do with the blood from the bull and the goat (vv. 14-15, 18-19)?

____

____

13. How often was the priest to make atonement (v. 34)?

____

14. List all of the things for which atonement was to be made in verses 30, 33-34.

____

____

In today's culture, it is hard to understand living during a time when animal sacrifice was a part of religious worship. To the children of Israel, however, this was God's chosen method for dealing with their sin. Just as we are repulsed by the thought of sacrificing an animal, we must remember that God is repulsed by our sin.

Let's take a closer look at the priest who makes atonement in Leviticus 16:32. We've printed this verse in bold from the New American Standard Bible and added our own emphasis in italic:

"So the priest who is *anointed* ..."

The word "messiah" comes from the Hebrew word "mashiach," which means "anointed."

"... and ordained to serve as priest *in his father's place* shall make *atonement*: ..."

Write out 1 John 4:14.

____

____

"... he shall thus put on the *linen* garments, the holy garments, and make atonement ..."

"And so they took the body of Jesus, and bound it in _________ ..." (John 19:40).

In referring to the feasts, Colossians 2:17 states that they "are a mere shadow of what is to come ..." Whose shadow do you see in the Leviticus 16:32 verse? ________________

Read Hebrews 7:26-28.

15. Record any new insight you have regarding these verses.

____

We are so thankful to have a perfect High Priest, one who is anointed: the Messiah. One who serves in His Father's place: the Son of God. One who atoned for us: the substance is Christ (Colossians 2:17).

The best entrance

Read Hebrews 9:1-10:18. This is the only reading for this section, so we would like to encourage you to take your time in reading this text and meditate on God's word.

1. What was in the outer part of the tabernacle called the holy place (9:2)?

____

2. What was in the holy of holies behind the second veil (9:3-4)?

____

3. What was in the Ark of the Covenant (9:4)?

____

4. Why didn't the sacrifices offered make the worshiper "perfect in conscience" (9:9-10)?

____

____

5. How did Christ enter the "greater and more perfect tabernacle" (9:11-12)?

____

6. How many times did He enter (9:12)?

____

7. What is the "greater and more perfect tabernacle" (9:24)?

____

8. How is the "Law" described in chapter 10, verse 1?

____

9. How have we been sanctified (10:10)?

____

During temple times, the high priest separated himself from his family for a week in preparation for the service he must render on the Day of Atonement. During this week, the other leaders of the law would go over with him exactly what was required of him for this day. On the Day of Atonement, he chose the lot to determine which goat was for the Lord and which was for the scapegoat. Then he tied the crimson wool on one of the goats. The high priest actually entered the Holy of Holies several times on this day. He offered the bull for a sin offering for himself and for his family, took coal from the altar where he offered that sacrifice, and carried it in the fire pan into the Holy of Holies. He then poured two handfuls of incense on the coals, got the blood of the bull which he had sacrificed, and returned to the Holy of Holies to sprinkle the blood on the mercy seat. He went back out, sacrificed the goat that was for the Lord and went back in and sprinkled this blood on the mercy seat. Then he left the mercy seat, mixed the bull's blood and goat's blood together, and sprinkled this on the horn of the altar. He would then go out, "lay both of his hands on the head of the live goat, and confess over it all the iniquities of the sons of Israel, and all their transgressions in regard to all their sins; and he shall lay them on the head of the goat and send it away into the wilderness by the hand of a man who stands in readiness. And the goat shall bear on itself all their iniquities to a solitary land; and he shall release the goat in the wilderness (Leviticus 16:21-22)."

What is really interesting about this little detail in Leviticus is that it is another notable "shadow" of Christ. When Yeshua took on our sins as the Passover Lamb, He was taken outside the city gates to be crucified. In fact, He was taken out by "the hand of a man who stands in readiness." Matthew 27:32, Mark 15:21, and Luke 23:26, all mention "a man of Cyrene named Simon, whom they pressed into service to bear His cross." Simon of Cyrene was the man who stood at the ready and led the "scapegoat" out into the "wilderness," in accordance with the foreshadowing established and woven into the Day of Atonement.

THE BEST ACCESS

In Leviticus 16:1 where we began this study, we looked at what was behind the veil and what was in the Ark of the Covenant. Let's take a closer look at the mercy seat on top of the ark.

Read Exodus 25:17-22.

1. Describe (or draw) the cherubim and their placement with regard to the mercy seat or atonement cover.

____

____

____

2. Where did God say He would meet with Moses (v. 22)?

____

Read John 20:11-12.

3. How many angels were in the tomb?

____

4. Where in the tomb were the angels?

____

Just like our credit card system covers our debt until the actual payment is made, the sacrificial system of the Old Testament covered sin until the ultimate payment was made with the blood of Jesus. The detail of where the angels were in the tomb seems insignificant, but this displays how Jesus' death was the fulfillment of the Old Testament sacrificial system. Even His tomb looked like the mercy seat that covered the Ark of the Covenant.

Furthermore, consider Psalm 99:1-3:

> *The LORD reigns,*
> *Let the nations tremble;*
> *He sits enthroned between the cherubim,*
> *Let the earth shake.*
> *Great is the LORD in Zion;*
> *He is exalted over all the nations.*
> *Let them praise your great and awesome name —*
> *He is holy* (NIV, International Bible Society, 1984).

The High Priest could only go beyond the veil to enter the Holy of Holies one day each year.

5. According to Matthew 27:51, what happened to the veil upon Jesus' death?

____

____

6. What do you think is the significance of this event?

____

____

7. In Acts 6:7, who were among those to believe as the "word of God kept on spreading"?

____

8. Why do you think this was?

____

____

The presence of God was above the mercy seat between the cherubim. From His view looking down onto the mercy seat, God saw the Law and how man was unable to keep it. On the Day of Atonement, He would have seen the blood from the sacrifices covering the Law. The blood showed that an innocent animal had given its life to temporarily atone for the sin of breaking the Law. After Jesus' death, God saw the blood of the perfect Lamb covering the Law. That is mercy!

In the garden when Adam and Eve sinned, an animal was killed for each of them to be clothed. Also, one animal was sacrificed in the place of Isaac on Mt. Moriah. On the day of Passover, a lamb was killed to save a *family*. On the Day of Atonement, an animal sacrifice made atonement for a *nation*. With the death of Jesus, the perfect Lamb of God was sacrificed to *save the world*! And now, because the veil has been torn, we are not limited to atonement and mercy only once each year. We now have forgiveness and free access to God through our High Priest, Jesus, anytime we want and as often as we desire.

Read Hebrews 4:14-16.

9. What privileges have we been given?

____

____

It is interesting that the priests were among those who believed. They probably understood, more than anyone, the symbolisms and recognized the substance of all those "shadows" set forth in the ancient scriptures to be that of Jesus. There were many laws pertaining to the priests, in particular. These ranged from not cutting the sides of their beards, set forth in Leviticus 21:5, to not having any specific defects listed in Leviticus 21:16-24.

In fact, when Dallas first read this extensive list of restrictions concerning the priests, it saddened her, specifically, that no man from their descendants with any defect, including disfigurement, could "come near to present the offerings made to the Lord by fire. He has a defect; he must not come near to offer the food of his God. He may eat the most holy food of his God, as well as the holy food; yet because of his defect, he must not go near the curtain or approach the altar, and so desecrate my sanctuary. I am the Lord, who makes them holy" (Leviticus 21:21-23 NIV).

This not only saddened her, but quite frankly, it made her mad at God. This seemed like a very mean requisite. If a man had been born in the lineage of a priest, his occupation as well as his lifestyle revolved around offering the sacrifices before the Lord. To be in this lineage and not to be able to go near the curtain or approach the altar must have been quite a disheartening feeling of failure.

Dallas was especially touched by this passage because her dad was born with a cleft palate. Had he been born in the line of the priest, he would not have been able to approach the altar or carry out his priestly duty. "That's not fair!" she thought. Her dad was a fantastic man who dearly loved God. He was kind, compassionate, and long-suffering. In fact, she contributes many of her understandings of the Heavenly Father and His love for her to her dad, because he showed her what a great dad is like.

When we were in Israel, we saw a little boy walking hand in hand with his father. They were both dressed in the black attire of the Hassidic Jew. As they passed, we saw the little boy glance up into his daddy's eyes, and we overheard just the beginning of the little boy's question, "Abba?" To hear that word spoken in that place blessed us in such a profound way. That is who God is to Dallas: "Abba," the daddy with all the answers, guiding her and holding her hand.

How then, could God disqualify these priests of old who had been born for the very purpose of bringing Him sacrifice just because of the way they looked or a defect they might have that was out of their control? Oh, what God would have missed not to have received offerings from someone like Dallas' dad! It seemed so unfair.

Then the last line of those Leviticus verses caught her attention. "I am the Lord, who makes them holy." God demands perfect holiness. A defect in a person is a direct result of a fallen world. Don't get us wrong, we don't mean that a person has defects because of their personal sin. To clarify, had there been no sin in the world, it would still be perfect. There would be no defect in anyone, no disease, no birth defects, no chromosomal abnormalities, and no cleft palates.

Dallas' grandmother used to tell her stories of all the teasing her daddy endured as a child because of his deformed lip. It broke her heart. She often thought, though, that it made her dad who he was. He loved everyone. He would have never dreamed of saying an unkind word to someone. He knew that hurt from his own experience and had no desire to inflict it upon anyone else. Had her dad been from a priestly lineage in the Temple times, why would God not desire him to come near the veil or to approach the altar? As she pondered these thoughts, the overwhelming reality hit her: this is exactly who God desires, and so He gave His only Son that her dad might approach the altar.

Never again would anyone be disqualified from offering a sacrifice of praise to the Holy Father based upon a physical defect. All of us have defects of the heart; none of us Gentiles have been born to the royal priesthood of Aaron, yet because of the loving Father who sacrificed His son, ALL can approach His altar. We have the best access available!

"Since then we have a great high priest who has passed through the heavens, Jesus the Son of God, let us hold fast our confession. For we do not have a high priest who cannot sympathize with our weaknesses, but one who has been tempted in all things as we are, yet without sin. Let us therefore draw near with confidence to the throne of grace, that we may receive mercy and may find grace to help in time of need" (Hebrews 4:14-16).

THE BEST SACRIFICE

The Jewish people today have several interesting customs associated with the Day of Atonement. The evening service that introduces Yom Kippur is called Kol Nidre (all vows). This is a formal cancellation of all vows made during the past year. It is also to ask for release from all vows that will be made in the coming year. This refers most specifically to religious vows, especially those made under duress. An example of this type of vow might be a person who has a personal crisis and cries out, "God, if you will get me out of this mess, I promise I will never miss another synagogue service as long as I live."

This tradition of Kol Nidre was more important in the days of forced "conversions" to Christianity when Jewish people might have to confess to be "Christian" to avoid torture or death, or they were forced to convert to Christianity. Kol Nidre is an opportunity to renounce that vow made under threat or coercion. In David H. Stern's book, *Restoring the Jewishness of the Gospel*, Stern explains that, "... 'converting to Christianity' is meant to be contrasted with 'becoming a Messianic Jew.' Jewish converts to Christianity and Messianic Jews both believe in Yeshua, but the latter retain their Jewish identity ... precisely what Jewish believers from the fourth century onward were often forbidden to do ... Actually, in the New Testament the term "Christian" is not used by believers to refer to Messianic Jews but to Gentiles who came to know the one true God through Yeshua the Jewish Messiah" (Stern, D. H., 1990, p. 7).

One of the traditional readings in today's synagogues on Yom Kippur is the book of Jonah. It reminds us to forgive others and not to think too highly of ourselves as it tells us that Jonah did not want God to forgive the people. This book is relevant for Yom Kippur (Day of Atonement), since it is a story of God's forgiveness of the people of Nineveh.

Because it is unlawful to carry money on Shabbat, Jews sell memberships to their synagogue rather than the Christian version of collecting money at their churches by "passing the plate." It is especially important that one has a place to sit in the synagogue on the Day of Atonement because the synagogue is usually crowded. Similar to church attendance on Easter and Christmas for some Christians, the Day of Atonement may be the only time all year that some Jews attend synagogue. Knowing this information gives us a better understanding of Jesus' frustration with the scribes and Pharisees in Matthew 23:5-6, when He confronts them about loving the place of honor and the "chief seats in the synagogues."

At the beginning of this chapter, we mentioned the ten Days of Awe preceding the Day of Atonement. These days are a time for seeking forgiveness from "sins against mankind," while the Day of Atonement is set apart particularly for sins committed against God, not for sins against individuals. Obviously, this day is observed differently now compared to temple times. After the destruction of the temple in 70 A.D., the focus of atonement was shifted from that of sacrifice to that of good works in order to obtain atonement. The justification for doing this comes from Hosea 6:6, "For I delight in loyalty rather than sacrifice, and in the knowledge of God rather than burnt offerings."

Some orthodox Jewish communities still partake in a ritual called Kapparot. On the day preceding Yom Kippur, the family gathers together. Each family member swings a chicken over their head and recites the following prayer: "This is my substitute, my vicarious offering, my atonement; this cock (or hen) shall meet death, but I shall find a long and pleasant life of peace." The fowls are then slaughtered and donated to the poor. (Money can be substituted for the chicken). The rabbis are quick to point out that this is not a sacrifice. Sacrifice is forbidden except in the temple. They would argue that it is a symbolic act of atonement. The point of using a chicken is to show the volatility of life. One minute the chicken is alive, the next minute it's not. If God had ruled by strict justice, our lives might go as fast as the chicken's! By the way, the chicken is not an animal that was ever sacrificed in temple times.

In our study of Passover, we learned about the word dayenu which means, "It is enough," or, "It would have been sufficient." Any Jewish person can quickly realize the Gentile background of this study by the fact that we include dayenu in a discussion on Yom Kippur. However, the concept of dayenu does indeed fit here. The Jews have set up a paradox. On one hand, the rabbis say sacrifice is not necessary for atonement. Good deeds and charity are enough; they are "dayenu." On the other hand, there is a ceremony involving a chicken being killed as a substitute. Is charity enough? Is blood sacrifice required? Which is it? We Gentiles, likewise, are responsible for attaching a few strings to the matchless grace that saves us. There is no substitute for the simplicity of the ultimate atoning sacrifice of Jesus. The Bible clearly teaches that forgiveness of sin requires the shedding of blood, and that the Messiah did that for us.

Read Leviticus 17:11.

1. What is it that makes atonement?

____

Read Hebrews 9:22.

2. Without the shedding of blood, there is no __________________

____.

Read Isaiah 64:5-6.

3. What is the role of works in being righteous before God? From God's point of view, what are our righteous acts?

____

____

It seems as if Isaiah is saying, "If you are expecting your righteous acts to make you worthy of God's forgiveness, forget it! When you bring your truckload of good deeds before God, He might say, 'What do I want with your filthy rags?'" When great men of the faith came into the presence of God, men like Abraham, Moses, Isaiah, and Elijah, they never said, "What a righteous person I am! I deserve to be in your presence." On the contrary, they were on their face, saying something akin to "I am not worthy. My righteous acts are like filthy rags."

Now, let's look at a New Testament view of good works. Read Ephesians 2:4-10.

4. What were we before God's mercy (v. 5)?

____

5. What saves us (v. 8)?

____

____

6. Why don't good works save us (v. 8-9)?

____

____

7. What is the role of good works (v. 10)?

____

____

Many churches today try to live within a similar paradox of what is required for forgiveness of sins. They preach that the sacrifice of Jesus *and* good works are needed for the removal of sin. But Jesus came as the perfect Lamb of God. While all of the Old Testament sacrifices were a temporary atonement for sin, they were only a shadow of the perfect sacrifice that would be made by Jesus. Jesus' sacrifice, on the other hand, was a sacrifice that did not merely atone for sin (cover it up), but removed sin. Is the sacrifice of Jesus enough ("dayenu") or not? We, as sinful people, cannot add anything to the perfect sacrifice of Jesus just by our works! The blood of Jesus, *dayenu*!

THE BEST RETURN

The Day of Atonement finds its fulfillment in the heart of a believer as he realizes a need for forgiveness of sin and recognizes that only the sacrifice made by Jesus can remove that sin. Yom Kippur also has a yet-to-be-realized, future fulfillment. We believe this will happen with the second coming of Christ. There are many Bible prophecies that point to this time. For instance, Hosea 3:4-5 tells us that the Jews will be set aside "for many days," but that a time will also come, "in the last days," when they will "return and seek their God and David their king."

Read Zechariah 14:4.

1. Where will Jesus return to the earth?

____

Read Zechariah 12:9-11.

2. What will the Lord do to the nations that come against Jerusalem (v. 9)?

____

____

3. What will the Lord pour out on the house of David (v.10)?

____

____

4. Who will they look upon?

____

5. Who is that person?

____

6. Why do you think they will mourn?

____

7. In Zechariah 13:9, the Jews call on the name of the Lord. God will say, "They are My people." What will be their reply?

____

Remember that the Day of Atonement is a most solemn occasion in which Jewish people fast and pray that they will be found acceptable for another year. Jewish people who may not observe any other service or feast during the rest of the year will probably observe the services of Yom Kippur. In 1973, the fact that so many Israelis were in synagogues observing Yom Kippur probably helped save their nation, since it facilitated a speedy mobilization of Israel's reserve troops when the country was surprise attacked by Egypt. "Thus, a nation at prayer rushed to the units and assembly areas, changing prayer shawls for battle kit on the way" (Herzog, 1984, p. 230). Israel would claim victory in this war that was later called the Yom Kippur War.

The closing prayers of the last service on Yom Kippur are the highlight of the day. Even though all have fasted throughout the day, many stand during this service. The Jewish writer, Blu Greenberg, in her book *How to Run a Traditional Jewish Household*, describes it this way:

> "Like most climaxes of life, there is a special tension, an almost palpable excitement that runs through the congregation. The prayers are quite beautiful. They are final pleas for mercy and blessing."
>
> "… The Shema Yisrael. 'Hear, O Israel, the Lord our God, the Lord is One,' is recited in full congregational voice. After this, the Baruch Shem K'vod, 'Praised be His name, Whose glorious kingdom is forever and ever,' is recited three times by the chazzan and congregation. And finally, the last declaration, 'The Lord is God' is recited, almost shouted out, seven times. After the seventh repetition there is a long, final blast of the shofar. As we often do at moments of intense feeling, we link ourselves to Zion and Jerusalem. Yom Kippur concludes with the congregational cry of *Lishanah ha'ba'ah be'yerushalayim*, 'Next year in Jerusalem.'"
>
> "The congregation has been together a full day through many peaks of emotion. There is much hugging and kissing and well-wishing. … In a few moments, the synagogue will be empty, everyone on the way home to break the fast and to begin preparations for Sukkot, which is only four days off" (Greenberg, 1983, p. 341).

In light of what you have just read about the traditional closing service on the Day of Atonement and taking into account that the Day of Atonement could be fulfilled with the Second Coming of Jesus, read Zephaniah 3:14-20. (You might also consider any other passages we have looked at in this section.)

Record any similarities you think are interesting or that you would like to remember.

____

____

____

____

____

____

____

____

____

____

Revelation 1:5-8 says, "… and from Jesus Christ, the faithful witness, the first-born of the dead, and the ruler of the kings of the earth. To Him who loves us, and released us from our sins by His blood, and He has made us to be a kingdom, priests to His God and Father; to Him be the glory and the dominion forever and ever. Amen. BEHOLD, HE IS COMING WITH THE CLOUDS, and every eye will see Him, even those who pierced Him; and all the tribes of the earth will mourn over Him. Even so. Amen. "I am the Alpha and the Omega," says the Lord God, "who is and who was and who is to come, the Almighty."

CHAPTER NINE

FEAST OF TABERNACLES (Sukkot)

— *A Lesson in Camping God's Way*

Carl opened the door to find our friend, Amy, standing there with an envelope. She seemed in a hurry to hand over the envelope, afraid we may not take it. Amy explained that there was money in it and that we shouldn't try to give it back to her. She felt like God was guiding her to give us this money, and she was only trying to be obedient.

Carl was in medical school at the time, and Dallas was staying home with our first child. We were living very frugally on a meager savings and on school loans. Amy was in a similar financial situation, we assumed, as she was a physical therapy student. As the saying goes, "We didn't have two nickels to rub together." We went to church with Amy, and she was aware of our hope for one last visit with Carl's sister, Margie, who was dying of cancer. Unfortunately, Margie lived halfway across the United States from us. Time off from medical school to make the drive wasn't an option, so the only possibility for the trip to see Margie was an expensive flight. Only Carl had planned to make the trip, but our home group surprised us by pitching in money to provide a ticket for Dallas to go, too. We were overwhelmingly thankful and felt prepared for the trip. Then Amy showed up at our door with more money.

Although we felt God had already provided so much for us through the generosity of our home group, it was hard to argue with Amy's strong feeling that God was guiding her to give us this money. Probably to her great relief, Carl very thankfully took the money. She did not want to be repaid, and she quickly left. When we opened the envelope, we found $100 inside.

In the days before Internet, if you needed to rent a car in another city, you made the reservation with a travel agent. Or, when you arrived at your destination, you picked up a courtesy phone in the airport lobby and started calling the rental car agencies listed on the advertising board by the phone. Being young, inexperienced travelers, we chose the latter. Unfortunately, every agency required a credit card and had a minimum age limit. We met neither requirement. As we tried the last number, Rent-A-Wreck, they gave us the same spiel about age and credit card. When Carl told them our predicament, they told him that they would be glad to forego those requirements if he had a $100 cash deposit. Thanks to God's guiding hand on Amy's obedient heart, we just happened to have $100 cash!

CAMPING WITH CLOUDS

As we will learn in this chapter, the Israelites were inexperienced travelers when they were camping in the desert, and they had no Internet, no call-ahead plans, and no nickels to rub together. They were completely at the mercy of God's guiding cloud by day and His pillar of fire by night (Exodus 13:21-22.) God is still in the business of guiding our lives. He dwells with us, meets our needs in unexpected ways, and uses us to bless others when we are obedient to His guidance.

Read Leviticus 23:39-44.

1. When was the Feast of Tabernacles supposed to be celebrated?

___

2. How long were they to celebrate this feast?

___

3. On what days were they to have a rest?

___

4. Why do you think they were to celebrate for seven days but have a rest on the eighth day?

___

5. Where were they to live for seven days?

___

6. What were they supposed to use to rejoice before the Lord (v.40)?

___

___

___

7. With what emotion do you think this occasion was to be observed? (Note the choice of verbs in verses 39-41.)

___

8. Why were the Israelites supposed to observe this feast (v. 43)?

___

___

In the chapters on Passover and Unleavened Bread, we learned that those feasts were set up so that the people would *remember* what God had done for them and how He delivered them from slavery. In the Feast of First Fruits, the purpose was *to celebrate being accepted.* God saved us from our bondage of sin, and Jesus, being the "First Fruit," allowed us to be accepted. At The Feast of Weeks, *all* people could participate. We, Gentiles, are grafted in, and a Comforter is given to all who believe. The Feast of Trumpets and the Day of Atonement provided for *forgiveness* from sin and from guilt, just as we have forgiveness through the Lamb of God.

Now, at the Feast of Tabernacles, the purpose is for *future generations to know* that God had the sons of Israel live in booths when He brought them out from the land of Egypt. We've come full circle from past to future. We remembered the past at Passover and Unleavened Bread, were accepted at First Fruits, received the Holy Spirit and forgiveness at Pentecost, Trumpets, and Day of Atonement, and now we are joyfully telling future generations of His guidance and provision at the Feast of Tabernacles. When the Son of the Living God lives in us — that is, "tabernacles" with us — we want all generations to know that He brought us out of our sin and bondage and gives us forgiveness and a Comforter. Let's celebrate and rejoice in the abundance of all God has provided for us!

The Feast of Booths (or Tabernacles) is a joyous occasion. The Day of Atonement has passed, and there is cause for celebration. Although Jews are commanded to celebrate this feast for seven days, instructions for rest and sacrifices are given concerning an eighth day. Today Jews celebrate this eighth day as a conclusion to the festival, even though this day is not technically called Tabernacles, or Sukkot.

This eighth day is called Shemini Atzeret which literally means "the assembly of the eighth (day)," but "atzeret" also has the meaning of "holding back" or of "stopping and waiting." The Jews have explained that God is like a king who has invited his children home to the palace. He enjoys them so much that when the time comes for them to leave, he invites them to stay one more day saying, "It is difficult for me to separate from you." Shemini Atzeret is a day to linger with the living God. Isn't this a wonderful thought! The God of the Universe doesn't want us to leave His presence. He desires more time with us, to linger with us. What a great illustration of love!

9. We often hear people talk about wanting to linger in the presence of God, but how does it change your perception of God to realize that He wants to linger with you?

____

____

____

____

____

Each of these last three feasts seems to have a prefillment in the life of a believer. We discussed the idea in the Feast of Trumpets that symbolically our soul hears the shofar of Jesus calling us to Him. On the Day of Atonement, we recognize Jesus as our High Priest, able to atone for our sins; and when we accept Him and His forgiveness, He comes into our hearts to live in (to tabernacle) with us. However, because we have seen a literal fulfillment in the feasts of Passover, Unleavened Bread, First Fruits, and Pentecost through Jesus and the Holy Spirit, it is reasonable to expect a literal fulfillment from these last three feasts as well.

In the previous two chapters, we discussed several possibilities for the fulfillments of the Feasts of Trumpets and the Day of Atonement. We believe the Feast of Tabernacles will most likely be fulfilled when "… the tabernacle of God is among men …" as Revelation 21:3 states. Therefore, let's look at the tabernacle and the temple to see what we can learn about the part these structures played in Israel's history. In ancient times, these were places God dwelt with His people.

Read Exodus 40:34-38.

10. How did the Israelites know the glory of the Lord filled the tabernacle (or tent of meeting)?

____

11. How did the cloud dictate their actions (vv. 36-37)?

____

____

12. When was the glory of the Lord with them (v. 38)?

____

____

It is so comforting to know that God is with us in all of our journeys both day and night, providing for our comings and goings, maybe through a cloud, as in ancient times, or by the blessing of a $100 bill obediently given to grieving, inexperienced travelers. He longs to provide for us, to spend time with us, just the same as we enjoy doing with our own children.

13. Give yourself some time this week to linger with the King. Linger in His word by meditating on Psalm 27. Write Him a prayer of thanksgiving or praise. Confide in Him your greatest fears or doubts.

____

____

____

____

____

____

____

We are so thankful that we can linger in God's word. The Jewish people are reminded of that blessing during this time as well. Another celebration associated with the "assembly of the eighth day" is Simkhat Torah. The annual cycle of weekly Torah readings is completed at this time.

The last Torah portion is read, followed immediately by the first chapter of Genesis. This is a reminder that the Torah is a circle and never ends, and the completion of the reading is a time of great celebration. As many people as possible, with plenty of fun singing and dancing, are given the honor of carrying the Torah scrolls around the synagogue. The name Simkhat Torah literally means "Rejoicing in the Torah."

KICKED OUT OF THE CAMPSITE

The Feast of Tabernacles is a great time of rejoicing, and while the Israelites were wandering in the desert, they had the blessing of the tabernacle and the presence of God with them. However, as Joshua led them into the promised land, although they were initially obedient, they quickly departed from following God. After Joshua died, the Israelites entered a dark period in their history. They fell away to idolatry and then suffered defeat at the hands of the other people groups in the land. The Israelites would finally cry out to God, and He would send them a "deliverer," or "judge," who would liberate them for a period of time. When the particular judge died, the people fell into idolatry again and the cycle repeated itself. This period of Israel's history is recorded in the book of Judges. Among some of the more familiar judges were Gideon, Samson, and Eli. Israel's last judge was Samuel.

In 1 Samuel 8:5, the Israelites told Samuel, "... Now appoint a king for us to judge us like all nations." Samuel prayed to God concerning this request and God answered him saying, "... for they have not rejected you, but they have rejected Me from being King over them" (1 Samuel 8:7). So God gave them what they asked. He led Samuel to anoint Saul as Israel's first king and later David as the second king. It was David's son Solomon who built the first temple in Israel.

Read 2 Samuel 7:1-2.

1. Why did David want to build God a house to dwell in?

____

____

Read 1 Kings 5:2-5.

2. Why didn't David build the temple for God?

____

____

3. Who built the first temple?

____

Read 1 Kings 8:2, 65-66.

4. What feast were they celebrating when they dedicated Solomon's Temple?

____

5. How long did they celebrate?

____

6. How did they leave on the day after this festival (the eighth day)?

____

____

Read 1 Kings 8:9-13.

7. What happened after the priests placed the ark in the Holy Place (vv. 10-11)?

____

____

According to 1 Kings 8:9, only the tablets were present in this ark; neither Aaron's rod that budded nor the golden jar of manna was present. These two articles are mentioned in Exodus 16:32-34 and in Numbers 17:10. Some people think that Aaron's rod and the jar of manna may have been lost between these two time periods, while others believe these two objects were never actually placed in the Ark of the Covenant but rather beside it. The Israelites began sacrificing in God's temple with a strict warning.

Read 1 Kings 9:1-9.

8. What did God tell them He would do if they turned away from following Him (v. 7)?

____

____

9. What would happen to the temple (v. 8)?

____

____

After Solomon's death, Israel had a "civil war" of sorts and was divided into a northern kingdom (calling itself Israel) and a southern kingdom (calling itself Judah). Throughout this period, both kingdoms basically obeyed God only to the extent that the reigning king obeyed God. We saw the positive influence King Hezekiah had on the southern kingdom (Judah) in our study on Unleavened Bread. Another notable king who "did right in the sight of the Lord" was King Josiah. However, God's patience with Israel's disobedience finally came to an end, and the king of Assyria invaded the land and carried Israel into exile. Not long after that, the same fate met the southern kingdom of Judah at the hands of King Nebuchadnezzar of Babylon.

Read 2 Chronicles 36:15-21.

10. What did the people do to bring on the wrath of the Lord (v.16)?

____

____

11. What happened to the temple (v.19)?

____

This happened in 586 B.C. Other accounts of the destruction of the temple appear in Jeremiah 52 and 2 Kings 25. The information given in 2 Kings says the destruction began on the 7th, and Jeremiah says it continued until the 10th. From this comes the 9th of Av, or Tish B'Av, which continues to be a Jewish day of fasting that commemorates the day of destruction of both the first and the second Temples. As we mentioned in the introduction of this book, the destruction of the second temple is believed to have been on the same day in 70 A.D.

Besides observing Tish B'Av, a couple of other notable reminders of the temple destruction are still a part of Jewish life. We learned about the roasted egg (slices of which were dipped in salt water at Passover) in the chapter on the Feast of First Fruits. Another tribute to this sadness at the loss of the temple occurs at Jewish weddings. Toward the end of the ceremony, a glass is wrapped in cloth and crushed beneath the groom's foot. This reminds those in attendance that even on such a joyous occasion as a wedding, there is still sorrow in the fact that there is no temple in which to sacrifice to God.

12. After the temple destruction, where were the "survivors" taken (v. 20)?

____

13. What characteristics of God do you see in verse 15?

____

____

____

14. What ways have you seen God display these characteristics for you in your life?

____

____

____

____

15. How have you responded?

____

____

____

____

We could probably learn a lot about our response to God from a man named Roger who Dallas' sister, Beverly, writes about:

> "Roger is one of those guys who looks like he's been through some rough times but has somehow managed to pull himself out of it enough to be able to function in the real world. He looks like he's in his sixties. He's got this wild grey hair that sticks out from under the cap he usually wears. He has black, horn-rimmed glasses, sometimes pushed up on his cap, sometimes riding on his nose like they are supposed to. He ALWAYS wears a shirt that says on the back "Roger Says PAY ATTENTION."
>
> I first saw Roger at a local football game three years ago. He was going up and down the stadium steps selling soft drinks. He had one of his shirts on and would yell out, "Pay attention! Drinks, three dollars!" and similar variations. I thought he looked a little intimidating, but I wondered about the PAY ATTENTION part. After that, I noticed he was selling drinks at all the games — high school and college, even the hockey games. Then one day the local paper mentioned him in a story about an anti-drug presentation made to some of the school students by a couple of prisoners from our local state prison. Roger had introduced the prisoners, and said that he, too, had experienced hard times, drug and alcohol use, jail time … you know the story. He had found religion and turned his life around. He told the kids to pay attention and stay away from drugs.

> I don't know what else Roger does to earn a living, but he's doing some good things for kids, and I think he's definitely paying attention to the way he is living each and every day, and that's something I need to remember to do. Pay attention. Every day" (Larson, 2009).

In 2 Chronicles 36:15, it is evident that God tried time and again to get the people's attention, but they were not obedient. God promised Solomon He would remove the people from their land and make the temple a heap of ruins. God did not disappoint. Jeremiah 25 contains the prophecy regarding the fall of Jerusalem at the hand of Nebuchadnezzar. That same prophecy declared that the children of Israel would serve Babylon for only seventy years. When their time of exile was over, God brought them back into their land and allowed His temple to be rebuilt.

Read Ezra 1:1-3.

16. Who appointed Cyrus to "build Him a house in Jerusalem"?

____

____

Read Ezra 3:1-13.

17. What is the name of the priest who helps build the altar as they again enter the promised land?

____

18. What feast did they first observe?

____

19. What other feasts did they observe?

____

20. Did they have a temple yet (v. 6)?

____

21. After the builders laid the foundation, what did the priests do (vv. 10-13)?

___

___

___

So much is happening in these verses. Priests are offering sacrifices with trumpets. Levites are praising and singing to the Lord with great shouts of praise because the foundation of the Lord has been laid. Look at this similar verse in Ephesians 2:19-22.

> *"So then you are no longer strangers and aliens, but you are fellow citizens with the saints, and are of God's household, having been built upon the foundation of the apostles and prophets, Christ Jesus Himself being the corner stone, in whom the whole building, being fitted together, is growing into a holy temple in the Lord; in whom you also are being built together into a dwelling of God in the Spirit."*

Our Cornerstone is Christ! Gentiles and Jews are fitted together to become a dwelling of God in the Spirit. Using the Ezra verses as a guide, our response should be shouts of praise and singing to the Lord.

22. What did the men who had seen the first temple think of this temple (Ezra 3:12-13)?

___

___

23. Explain why you think there were different emotions on this occasion.

___

___

___

___

24. How have you allowed Jesus to be the foundation of your life?

____

25. What size "temple" can be built on your foundation?

____

____

At the completion of the second temple, the people had many different emotions. Some of them may have been sad that this temple was so much smaller than the last. Some may have just been glad to have a temple again. Likewise, today, people have different emotions when they ask Christ to "tabernacle" with them and to be the Lord of their lives.

Dallas remembers her daddy (also named Dallas) sharing his experience of asking Jesus to live in his heart. He was a youngster when he realized his need for forgiveness. The church he attended with his parents had a tradition of inviting people to walk to the front if they wanted to let other people know of their decision to believe in Jesus. It was a serious time for Dallas' daddy, and he cried as he walked forward, fully acknowledging his need for forgiveness and for a Savior. The next day some of his classmates, who also attended his church, made fun of him for crying. He told them that he wasn't ashamed of crying, and if they had experienced the same forgiveness and love that he had, they would have cried, too.

Probably some of those older priests who wept when the foundation of the Lord was laid experienced the forgiveness and restoration of God's love personally just as Dallas' daddy did. They may have been reminded of their disobedience that led to their captivity in the first place and experienced great emotion at the fact that they would now have a temple to seek forgiveness as the law prescribed. Others may have looked forward joyfully to the future of a new homeland and an opportunity to serve the Lord in freedom.

CLEANING THE TENT

The re-gathering of Israel to the promised land and the rebuilding of the temple began what was known as the Second Temple Period. This second temple was not of the magnitude of Solomon's temple. Ezra 6:5 records that the gold and silver utensils taken from the first temple by Nebuchadnezzar were returned and placed in the Second Temple. One major item that was not present in the second temple, however, was the ark of the covenant.

The absence of the ark of the covenant is noteworthy since the statement from King David as to why he wanted to build the temple in the first place was because "the ark of God dwells within tent curtains" (2 Samuel 7:2). The main reason Solomon built the first temple was for a place for God's Spirit to dwell.

The last time the ark of the covenant is mentioned in scripture is when King Josiah (623 B.C.) orders the ark to be put back in the temple (2 Chronicles 35:3). Possibly during the reign of wicked kings, the priests took the ark out of the temple and hid it away somewhere. There is no further mention of the ark in the biblical record after this, but it does not seem likely that the ark was destroyed by the Babylonians in 586 B.C., as such a calamity would certainly have been mentioned. When the second temple was rebuilt in the time of Ezra, the ark was not returned to the temple. The Holy of Holies presumably remained empty until the destruction of Herod's Temple in 70 A.D. Indeed, according to Josephus, a first-century Jewish historian, the inner chamber of the temple was completely empty: "In this stood nothing whatever: unapproachable, inviolable, invisible to all, it was called the Holy of Holy" (Josephus, p. 856).

During the time of Rehoboam (927-911 B.C.), 2 Chronicles 12:9 says, "So Shishak King of Egypt came up against Jerusalem and took away the treasures of the house of the Lord and the treasures of the King's house, he took all away." Notice that he took *all* away; this may have included the ark of the covenant.

When the temple was rebuilt, many thought that the ark would be returned to the second temple's Holy of Holies. But, according to *Where is the Ark of the Covenant?* by Arthur Edward Bloomfield, "When the Roman General Pompey conquered Jerusalem around 63 B.C., he demanded the privilege of entering the Holy of Holies. When he did, he came out saying that he could not understand what all the interest was about the sanctuary, when it was only an empty room" (Bloomfield).

Read Haggai 2:1-9.

1. How did the second temple compare to the first temple (v. 3)?

____

____

2. What does God promise in verse 9?

____

____

3. Why do you think the glory of the second temple was greater than the first temple?

____

____

By the time of Jesus, Judea was ruled by Rome, and Herod was its Roman ruler. The second temple became known as Herod's temple. Herod was recognized for his great building projects. He modified and rebuilt the second temple in such a way that many people consider Herod's temple to be the "third temple." This work began in 19 B.C. The main buildings were finished by 9 B.C., but the work was not completed until 64 A.D. Herod actually died in 4 B.C. before the work on the temple was finished. It was this temple that was present during the time of Jesus. Maybe the glory of the second temple was greater because Jesus actually walked in it. Even though there was no ark of the covenant, the presence of God was in this temple in the person of Jesus. Let's see what Jesus had to say about the temple.

Read John 2:13-22.

4. During what festival does this event take place?

____

5. Why did Jesus drive out the moneychangers?

____

____

____

Money changers were needed because the Jews could not use money in the temple if it had the image of a man on it. (Current Israeli coins, New Shekels, still hold to this rule of not having a person's image on them.) Since the Roman money (a denarius) had a picture of Caesar on it, they could not use it in the temple. They had to use temple money (a shekel). A place to exchange one for the other was a must. The problem was that the money changers were illegally profiting from this exchange. (Ritmeyer, 2002, p. 27).

Ancient Roman coin

New Shekels

6. What did Jesus say as a sign to show his authority to cleanse the temple (v. 19)?

____

____

7. What temple was Jesus talking about (v. 21)?

____

Jesus rebuked the moneychangers in the temple on two occasions. One was at the beginning of His ministry and one was at the end. Both occurrences were during the Passover.

Read Luke 19:37-48.

8. What was the crowd saying as Jesus approached the city (v. 38)?

____

____

Remember from our study on the bridegroom in the chapter on Passover that this same blessing, "Blessed is He who comes in the name of the Lord," is still recited at weddings as the bridegroom enters. Another interesting observation here is that, once again, both jubilant and sorrowful emotions are present. Jesus wept over the city while the disciples joyfully praised God.

9. What did Jesus prophesy about the temple in verse 44?

____

____

10. Why was this going to happen?

____

____

Read Matthew 23:37-39.

11. What did Jesus want to do for Jerusalem?

____

____

12. How would the temple be left?

____

13. What will Jerusalem say when they see Jesus again (v. 39)?

____

____

It is very probable that Jesus entered Jerusalem through the Eastern Gate amid shouts of hosanna. The Eastern Gate was the only gate that led directly onto the Temple Mount.

Let's look forward to a time when Jesus again will enter the Eastern Gate.

Read Ezekiel 43:1-9.

14. From where was the glory of God coming (vv. 2, 4)?

____

____

15. What did His voice sound like?

____

16. What happened in the temple (v. 5)?

____

Read Ezekiel 44:1-2.

17. What happened to the Eastern Gate?

____

The following is an excerpt from an article by Dr. David R. Reagan (used with permission):

> "The Eastern Gate in the old walled city of Jerusalem has a very special place in my heart, for it was that gate which God used to open my eyes to His Prophetic Word. The year was 1967. The occasion was the Six Day War. As the fate of the new state of Israel hung in the balance, I searched the newspapers daily for any information I could find about the war. The turning point came on June 7 when the Israeli army broke through the Lion's Gate and returned control of the ancient city of Jerusalem to the Jewish people for the first time in 1,897 years.
>
> The next day I read a fascinating news account about one of the Jewish commando groups that had been involved in the assault on the city. The article stated that some members of the group had suggested catching the Jordanian defenders of the city off guard by blowing open the sealed Eastern Gate. But the leader of the group, an Orthodox Jew, had vehemently protested the idea, stating that 'the Eastern Gate can be opened only when the Messiah comes …'
>
> … My concordance quickly directed me to the passage that the Orthodox Jew had alluded to. I found it in Ezekiel 44. The context is a supernatural tour the Lord is giving Ezekiel of the future Millennial Temple (40:1-3).
>
> In chapter 43, the Lord gives Ezekiel a vision of God's glory entering the Millennial Temple from the east, through the Eastern Gate. The Lord then says to Ezekiel: "Son of Man, this is the place of My throne and the place of the soles of my feet where I will dwell among the sons of Israel forever" (43:7).

The Lord then reveals to Ezekiel that the Eastern Gate will be closed and will not be reopened until the Messiah returns in glory (44:1-3).

This prophecy was partially fulfilled more than 400 years ago in 1517 when the Turks conquered Jerusalem under the leadership of Suleiman the Magnificent. He commanded that the city's ancient walls be rebuilt, and in the midst of this rebuilding project, for some unknown reason, he ordered that the Eastern Gate be sealed up with stones.

Legends abound as to why Suleiman closed the Gate. The most believable one is that while the walls were being rebuilt, a rumor swept Jerusalem that the Messiah was coming. Suleiman called together some Jewish rabbis and asked them to tell him about the Messiah. They described the Messiah as a great military leader who would be sent by God from the east. He would enter the Eastern Gate and liberate the city from foreign control.

Suleiman then decided to put an end to Jewish hopes by ordering the Eastern Gate sealed. He also put a Muslim cemetery in front of the Gate, believing that no Jewish holy man would defile himself by walking through a Muslim cemetery.

The Gate has remained sealed since that time. The Muslim cemetery still blocks the entrance. The old walled city has eight gates; and the Eastern Gate, and it alone, is sealed — just as prophesied in Ezekiel 44. The world would call that an 'amazing coincidence.' I call it a 'God-incidence.'

The Eastern Gate is proof positive that the Bible is the Word of God. Its sealing is clear evidence that we are living in the end times. The Gate awaits the return of the Messiah. Then and only then, will it be opened" (Reagan, 1998, p. 6).

EASTERN GATE, 2010

The psalmist writes in Psalm 118:19-20, "Open to me the gates of righteousness; I shall enter through them, I shall give thanks to the Lord. This is the gate of the Lord; the righteous will enter through it." Psalm 118 is a part of the Hallel that is a traditional reading still observed today both at Passover and at the Feast of Tabernacles. In our study on Passover, we read through the Hallel, noting any references to the Messiah, especially as they related to Passover. Keeping in mind what you've learned about the Feast of Tabernacles, read Psalm 118:10-29.

18. What references do you notice that have some relation to the Feast of Tabernacles?

____

____

It is with great joy that we look forward to entering the gates of righteousness with the Lord!

CAMPING WITH CHRIST

We have looked at a quick history of the temple in the past few sections. Remember that the first feast celebrated when the Israelites returned to rebuild the second temple was the Feast of Booths (Tabernacles.) The New Testament records a Sukkot (Tabernacles) festival that Jesus celebrated.

Read John 7.

1. Why wasn't Jesus in Judea?

____

2. What feast was being celebrated?

____

3. Why do you think the brothers of Jesus wanted Him to go to Jerusalem for the feast (vv. 3-5)?

____

____

4. Why did Jesus go "in secret" to the feast?

____

5. When and how did Jesus make himself known to those celebrating in Jerusalem (v. 14)?

____

6. Jesus credited his knowledge to whom?

____

7. What can we learn from Jesus about testing the validity of a teacher (vv.17-18)?

____

____

8. From verses 40 and 41, what do you think the difference is between "the Prophet" and "the Christ"?

____

As we studied Passover, we learned about the Cup of Elijah and the belief among the Jews that Elijah would precede the Messiah. This could have been a reference to that belief. Also, in Deuteronomy 18:15, Moses prophesies that "The Lord your God will raise up for you a prophet like me from among you, from your countrymen; you shall listen to him." So this statement in John 7 could also be a reference to their understanding of that scripture in the Torah. We believe the prophecy of Moses concerning a future prophet was pointing to Jesus. Moses was a type of Christ, as we see this comparison made in Hebrews 3:1-2: "Therefore, holy brethren, partakers of a heavenly calling, consider Jesus, the Apostle and High Priest of our confession. He was faithful to Him who appointed Him, as Moses also was in all His house."

When we contrast John 7:27 with John 7:40-42, we also notice a contradiction on the part of the crowd. Some claimed no one would know where the Messiah would come from, while others rightly acknowledged that, according to the Tanakh, the Messiah would come from Bethlehem and be the offspring of David. These differing ideas attributed to the division in the crowd, leading to the Pharisees' frustration in John 7:49. However, it seems apparent that at least some members of the crowd were impressed on some level with this man from Galilee, as stated in John 7:31. Jesus seeks to clarify His identity in His emphatic statement, crying out loudly on the last day of the feast.

9. What statement does Jesus make in John 7:37-38?

____

____

10. When does He declare this (v. 37)?

____

11. How is the Spirit described (vv. 38-39)?

____

During Jesus' time, a water ritual was observed by the priests. On each of the seven days of the Feast of Tabernacles, the priests dipped water from the pool of Siloam, which was literally in the shadow of the temple. They brought the water to the altar and poured it out as an offering to the Lord. This water procession was celebrated with great joy and rejoicing, as stated in Isaiah 12:3, "Therefore you will joyously draw water from the springs of salvation." On the seventh and last day of the feast, the priests circled the altar seven times and then poured out the water on the altar. This partially represented thanking God for the upcoming winter rains, but on a spiritual level it celebrated Isaiah 12:2-3. Isn't it a startling eye-opener that this Jewish water ritual celebrated with joy the same salvation that we Christians celebrate during our worship together?

12. In light of this water celebration, what impact do you think Jesus' statement in John 7:37-38 had on those who heard it?

____

Read Isaiah 12:1-6.

13. Because God is our strength, song, and salvation, what will we be able to do (v. 3)?

____

In this chapter of Isaiah, the pronoun "you" changes from masculine singular in verse 1 to masculine plural in verse 3, to finally feminine plural in verse 6, perhaps suggesting the timeline of acceptance of the Messiah by the world. The masculine singular may suggest personal praise and acceptance of the Lord for salvation as outlined in verses 1-2, while the shift to masculine plural may invite Israel corporately (maybe as happened at the Feast of Tabernacles in John 7) to joyously draw water from the "springs of salvation," enabling them to give thanks and call on His name "in that day" (meaning the last days). And, finally, feminine plural proposing the idea that the "Holy One of Israel" will be in the midst of the inhabitants of Zion, all believers in the Messiah - the Bride of Christ! Are you drinking deeply from the living water that is Christ our Lord?

Read Zechariah 14:8-21. These verses tell us more about what will happen "in that day" after Christ returns and sets up His Kingdom.

14. What will flow out of Jerusalem? And where will it flow?

____

____

15. When will the events of this passage take place (vv. 8-9)?

____

____

16. Who will the Lord strike with the plague (vv.12-15)?

____

____

17. What will the people who are left do (v.16)?

____

____

18. What will happen to those who do not go up to worship (vv.17-18)?

____

____

19. What do you think is significant about even the horses' bells and people's cooking pots being holy to the Lord (vv. 20-21)?

____

____

In that day, *everything* will be holy to the Lord, and we will celebrate the Feast of Tabernacles with the Lord of Hosts. Oh, let us quench our thirst now! How grateful we are that we don't have to wait, but that we can drink of the Lord's goodness in this present time! Praise Him for showering us with His salvation!

Campsite etiquette

We excitedly anticipate the fulfilling of the Feast of Tabernacles. Since we have seen Passover, Unleavened Bread, First Fruits, and Pentecost literally fulfilled by Jesus and the Holy Spirit, it's logical that the next three will be literally fulfilled. They are fulfilled to some degree in the life of the believer. The shofar (Feast of Trumpets) calls our heart toward God. We realize our need for forgiveness, sacrifice, and a High Priest mediator (Day of Atonement). Then, in accepting Christ as the perfect sacrifice for our sin, He promises to "tabernacle" with us (Feast of Tabernacles) and is the king of our heart. Dayenu (it is enough). But there is more:

Read Zechariah 6:12-13.

1. Who will build the temple of the Lord?

____

2. What "two offices" will He hold?

____

Jesus of Nazareth literally means "Yeshua, or Joshua the Branch," or "salvation from branch-land." Also, Jesus has the distinction of being called both a high priest and a king. In Hebrews 5, Jesus is compared to Melchizedek. We know that Melchizedek was both a priest and a king from Genesis 14:18-20. When Jesus returns to this earth, He will deliver Israel from all the nations that have come against them. And He will reign as King of Kings and Lord of Lords!

Read Revelation 21:1-27.

3. What is the first phrase the voice from the throne says in verse 3?

____

____

4. What does He promise those who are thirsty in verse 6?

____

____

5. Who will inherit these things?

____

Read 1 John 5:4-5 and Revelation 3:12.

6. From these verses, write out a definition for an "overcomer."

____

____

Read Revelation 22:1-7, 12-14. Notice that there is no temple in this glorious city of Jerusalem, for the Lord God the Almighty and the Lamb are its temple.

7. What is coming from the throne of God and of the Lamb?

____

____

8. When is Jesus coming (v.12)?

____

____

9. What is the promise for believers in verse 14?

____

____

We have observed a number of significant aspects of the history of the tabernacle and the temples throughout this study. By filling in the chart below, we can see some interesting similarities that tie them all together.

Use the following scripture references to complete the chart.

SCRIPTURE	SIGHT AND SOUND	EVENT/PLACE
Exodus 19:16-19	Thunder, lightning, thick cloud, trumpet, smoke, fire, earthquake	
Exodus 40:34-38		Glory of the Lord filled the tabernacle
1 Kings 8:10-12		God's presence in Solomon's temple
Acts 2:1-4	Violent rushing wind, tongues of fire	
Revelation 4:1-5		God's presence in the throne room
Revelation 19:6-9		Marriage supper of the Lamb, Second Coming of Christ
Ezekiel 43:1-7		Glory filled the house — Millennial Temple

God's manifestation of His presence is so consistent throughout time and throughout His word. His presence and power are available to us, since we are His temple until He returns again. Revelation 22:20 says, "He who testifies to these things says, 'Yes, I am coming quickly.' Amen. Come, Lord Jesus." While we wait for our Lord to come quickly, we can celebrate that we are a temple of God and the Spirit of God dwells in us (1 Corinthians 3:16). The Jews also are awaiting their Messiah. Let's see what we can learn from how they celebrate the Feast of Tabernacles today.

The Feast of Booths is an extremely joyous occasion, since the time of fasting and solemn assembly from the Day of Atonement is over. Today, as they are commanded in Leviticus 23, the Jews build booths (Sukkot) for the seven-day festival. After the Day of Atonement, they have five days to build their sukkah. It must be a temporary structure, with at least two complete walls and a part of a third wall. It is acceptable to use existing walls, such as the outside walls of a house or fence. The roof, however, must be made of plant material and be rebuilt every year.

The roof must be sufficiently covered so that it gives more shade than sun during the daytime. Yet it should be sufficiently open so that the stars are visible through the roof at night. Since the sukkah is supposed to be like your home for seven days, some people decorate it by hanging fruit from the ceiling or putting posters of Jerusalem or Jewish-themed pictures on the walls. Jewish people feel that if they are dwelling in a sukkah, the presence of God is dwelling with them as if they have been invited to enter the holy place of God. The Talmud says that in the days of the Messiah, all Jews will dwell together in one gigantic sukkah.

In Leviticus 23:42, God commands the Israelites to live in booths for seven days. If the Jews are unable to actually live in their Sukkot, they will at least eat a meal there. This meal is usually eaten on the first night of the feast. Rabbis have explained that the time in the sukkah is not intended to be unpleasant. If time spent in the sukkah is too uncomfortable (because of rain or cold for instance), the participants are allowed to go back into their houses, because if one is preoccupied with discomfort, that person will miss the whole point of sukkah, which is joy.

As with all of the Jewish feasts, there is a great deal of symbolism in the Feast of Booths, and the whole exercise serves as a great object lesson. We have a tendency to place our trust in our possessions, which gives us a false sense of security. God wants us to trust only in Him. By asking the Jews to leave the security of their houses and live in temporary shelters, God gives them an opportunity to realize that possessions are temporary. It is during this time of being separated from worldly possessions and comforts that God commands the Jews to find joy in Him.

10. What are your greatest possessions in life?

____

11. What are you lacking? Can you enjoy life without those things you're lacking?

____

____

12. How would you react to losing your most prized possession(s)?

____

____

Another observance related to Sukkot involves what is known as The Four Species or the lulav and etrog. The Jews are commanded to take these four plants and use them to rejoice before the Lord. The etrog (or citron) is a citrus fruit, resembling a lemon that is native to Israel. The lulav is made of a palm branch, two willow branches, and three myrtle branches bound together. These four species are waved in all six directions (north, east, south, west, up, and down) to symbolize that God is everywhere. The four species are also held during the Hallel prayer in religious services and during processions around the bimah (the pedestal where the Torah is read) each day during this holiday. These processions commemorate the water processions around the altar performed during the temple period that we discussed earlier. The processions are known as Hoshanahs, because while the Jews walk around the bimah, they recite a prayer with the refrain, "Hoshana!" (Please save us!).

Tradition teaches that the four species are symbolic of four types of Jews:

> 1) The etrog (citron), which has a fragrance and a taste, represents those Jews who have both Torah wisdom and good deeds.
>
> 2) The lulav (date palm branch) which has a taste (from the dates), but no fragrance, represents those Jews who have Torah wisdom, but no good deeds.
>
> 3) The myrtle branches have a fragrance, but no taste, representing those Jews who have good deeds, but no Torah wisdom.
>
> 4) The willow branches have neither a taste nor a smell, representing those Jews who are lacking in Torah wisdom and good deeds.

13. Which of these four species best represents your life in service to the "King of the Jews"?

____

As we have considered throughout this chapter how this feast may be fulfilled, it is our opinion that the Second Coming of Jesus will ultimately fulfill this feast. As we read in Revelation 21:3-7, "… "Behold, the tabernacle of God is among men, and He shall dwell among them, and they shall be His people, and God Himself shall be among them, and He shall wipe away every tear from their eyes; and there shall no longer be any death; there shall no longer be any mourning, or crying, or pain; the first things have passed away.' And He who sits on the throne said, 'Behold, I am making all things new.' And He said, 'Write, for these words are faithful and true.' And He said to me, 'It is done. I am the Alpha and the Omega, the beginning and the end. I will give to the one who thirsts from the spring of the water of life without cost. He who overcomes shall inherit these things, and I will be His God and he will by My son.'"

LULAV AND ETROG

If the Feast of Tabernacles is when Jesus again returns to this earth as a reigning king, consider the significance of what the Jews will be doing on that day. On the eve of the seventh day of the feast, the Jews still pray for water. They understand they need water to live. And on the eighth day, Shemini Atzeret, they continue to pray for rain. From the eighth day of this feast until Passover, they will insert the following phrase in their synagogue service, "[God] Who brings the winds and causes the rain to fall," just before the resurrection blessing, "Blessed are You, God, Who restores life to the dead."

"Rain is compared to resurrection because it, too, brings forth from the ground life which has been barren or 'dead' since the last harvest. The Rabbis suggest that rain is as miraculous as resurrection" (Greenberg, 1983, p. 367). Indeed, the One Who claimed to quench the thirst of all those willing to come to Him for a drink will, on that last day of the Feast of Tabernacles we read about in John 7, bring resurrection to the dead and restore life!

And, on this eighth day of Shemini Atzeret, He will linger with us. The Bridegroom is coming to linger with us, to wipe away every tear! He is the "root and the offspring of David, the bright morning star. And the Spirit and the bride say, 'Come.' And let the one who hears say, 'Come.' And let the one who is thirsty come; let the one who wishes take the water of life without cost" (Revelation 22:16-17).

Come quickly, Lord. Be our shower of comfort, our deluge of joy. Drench us with peace and hope and love, that our faith may finally be a feast of "praise and glory and honor at the revelation of Jesus Christ; and though you have not seen Him, you love Him, and though you do not see Him now, but believe in Him, you greatly rejoice with joy inexpressible and full of glory, obtaining as the outcome of your faith the salvation of your souls" (1 Peter 1:7-9).

This beautiful picture of resurrection and abundant eternal life concludes the study of the seven feasts of Israel as set up by God in Leviticus 23. In the next chapter, we will look at the Feasts of Hanukkah and Purim. These are two feasts (of several) that Jews observe to remember important events in their history. They were not set up by God as feasts to celebrate every year. However, they do have Biblical significance, and we as Christians can learn a great deal from them. In fact, one of them is mentioned in the New Testament, and it is fairly apparent that Jesus observed it as well.

CHAPTER TEN

PURIM/HANUKKAH

— *A Lesson on Time and Place*

Purim

In the hostile land of ancient Persia, one woman's courageous voice brings hope and amazing grace to her people — long, long ago, and once again today.

In modern-day Iran, once known as Persia, the current political climate is as cruel and unforgiving as it ever was under the rule of the ancient Persian kings. Currently, Americans are not encouraged to travel there. However, our friend Susan recently returned from a journey to pray for and inspire fellow believers living in Iran. Susan's party covertly shared some Bibles along the way and offered encouragement to believers in a couple of above-ground churches while traveling as an inconspicuous group with an official Iranian tour guide. One of their sightseeing locations included a mosque. As they toured it, the guide informed them of a special location within the mosque that acoustically enhances a person's voice as if speaking into a microphone. The guide urged one of them to stand at the spot and give it a try. One woman in Susan's group walked to the particular place in the vacant mosque, dropped her hands, tilted back her head and began to sing the words to an old hymn. In a faraway land of unbelievers in the God of Israel, under the watchful eye and listening ear of a government official, one courageous woman offered a prayer of hope and a testimony to her own journey as the words she sang were amplified and echoed gloriously throughout the mosque, carried away on the melody to listeners in the street beyond, "Amazing grace, how sweet the sound, that saved a wretch like me …".

This isn't the first time one woman's voice, with a lot of prayer and a little courage, brought the hope of amazing grace to the troubled land of Persia. A woman of immense faith had been there many years before. Hers is the great story of Purim.

Such a great story!

Purim is a feast that celebrates the deliverance of Israel from destruction at the hands of Haman. This occurred during the first dispersion of the Jews. The Jews were in Persia, which is modern day Iran, around 450 B.C. The Israelites had been given permission to return to Israel and rebuild the temple, but the majority of Jews stayed in Persia with no desire to return to the promised land. The book of Esther records the events of this time.

Take a few minutes to grab your favorite Bible and read the book of Esther. Yes, the whole book! (No whining, now. It is only ten chapters long.) Actually, it has a great plot and a story line that would rival any modern short story. We think you will greatly enjoy reading it.

Such a time as this!

We hope you enjoyed reading the story of Esther. Did you notice that God is not mentioned even once in this book? It is amazing how evident God's presence and protection is on His chosen Jewish nation even though He is not mentioned by name.

1. Take a minute to reflect on circumstances in your life that demonstrate the "hand of God" guiding and protecting you, even though you are not able to literally see Him or hear His voice. Jot down one of your experiences.

___

___

___

In the first ten years of our marriage, we moved six times and lived in four different cities. We really had very little control of any of these situations. Each one of the moves was chosen for us due to our education requirements or a job obligation. We didn't get to choose the city, and on one occasion, we didn't choose the house either. We rented it over the phone and hadn't even seen it until we pulled up in the moving truck to move in our belongings. At that time, we had two small children, and it was a little stressful moving across the country to a strange house and unfamiliar neighborhood. However, we received comfort from knowing that God had a hand in our move. Carl likes to say, "When God's moving truck pulls up to the curb, you start loading boxes."

After the sixth move in our marriage, we were blessed to stay put for five years. We began to desire a little more room as our fourth child was on the way. We didn't need the extra space; we just wanted it. It was the first time in fifteen years of marriage we could decide for ourselves if we wanted to move or not. Although it would be a move within the same town, our children's school would change, and we would be leaving great neighbors. It was a hard decision. We longed for the confirmation of God's moving truck pulling up in the driveway.

We found a house to buy, but needed to sell ours first. Dallas thought that maybe confirmation on the move could come in the form of selling our house. We had a couple of strikes against us for a quick sale. We wanted to sell it ourselves, without the help of a realtor. We wanted to sell it within two weeks, which also happened to be over the Christmas holiday. And, we had personalized the house to the extent that our sons' room had their names, Connor and Carson, painted on the wall. Carl was somewhat skeptical of the sale of the house happening within Dallas' timeframe, even joking that no one was going to buy a house with "some kid's name painted on a wall." Dallas laughingly replied, "We serve a big God! If we're supposed to move, I think He can find someone to buy the house who has sons named Connor and Carson."

We put the house on the market over the Christmas holidays just as it was. We started packing boxes — and closed the deal on the house one month later. The buyer's only request was that we paint over Carson's name and re-paint the "o" in Connor's name to an "e" because they loved the room, but they spelled their son's name C-O-N-N-E-R!

When God's moving truck pulls up to the curb, we have assurance that our heavenly home will be all that we've hoped for even if we haven't seen it firsthand, and we will live forever with the One Who has our names, not just painted on a bedroom wall, but written in the Book of Life (Luke 10:20) and on the very palm of His hands! Let us proclaim His amazing grace for the entire world to hear!

It is so fun, and such an encouragement to our faith, when we see God work in our lives. Let's take a closer look at how God worked in Esther's life. To better understand the book of Esther, it is helpful to know the historical context. After Solomon's temple was destroyed in 586 B.C. by King Nebuchadnezzar, the Jews were taken into captivity. In 538 B.C., the Edict of Cyrus allowed the Jews to return to Jerusalem and rebuild the temple. The events of Esther occurred about 475 BC. Many Jews had already returned to Jerusalem. Thousands of Jewish citizens chose to remain in Persia, probably because this had become home to them during their long separation from their native land. Thus, the book of Esther shows clearly that God protects His chosen people, even when they are scattered among the nations of the world.

To enhance your knowledge a little, answer the following questions from the book of Esther.

2. Mordecai was a descendant of what tribe (2:5)?

____

3. How was Esther related to Mordecai (2:5-7)?

____

____

4. Why did Esther keep her Jewish heritage a secret (2:10)?

____

____

5. Why did Haman hate Mordecai (3:2-5)?

____

____

6. What was Haman's solution for dealing with Mordecai (3:6-8)?

____

____

____

____

7. From Esther 3:1, what nationality was Haman?

____

Haman was a descendant of Agag, who was an Amalekite. Remember from question number 2 that Mordecai was a Benjamite. Let's take a quick side trip to learn more about prior confrontations between the Amalekites and the Benjamites.

1 Samuel 10:20-22 describes how Saul, a Benjamite, was chosen as Israel's first king.

Read 1 Samuel 15:1-11.

8. Who was Saul supposed to destroy (v. 3)?

____

9. Whom did he spare (v. 8)?

____

God removed the kingdom from Saul because of his disobedience. If Saul had obeyed God, the Amalekites would not have survived. Haman would not have existed. The story of Esther is an example of how one generation's disobedience can affect future generations.

10. What disobedience or habit might you be responsible for that could affect future generations of your family? How will you change it?

____

____

11. Why was Esther reluctant to go before the king and "plead for her people" (4:7-11)?

____

____

12. How did Mordecai respond to Esther when he learned that she did not want to go before the king (4:13-14)?

____

____

____

____

____

13. What did Esther ask the Jews to do before she approached the king (4:15-17)?

____

____

____

____

14. Why do you think she made this request?

____

____

15. List some of the positive character traits you observed in Esther.

____

____

____

____

It's interesting to note the difference in Esther's obedience to God and Saul's disobedience to God in not destroying the Amalekites. We know that Esther found favor with the king and interceded on behalf of her people. Through Esther, God was able to turn a seemingly hopeless situation into a time of great joy and victory for the Jews.

One of the awesome things about God is that while He shows Himself faithful to a nation, He is also faithful and compassionate to us individually. He was so kind to Esther in providing her with the knowledge that prayers were being offered on her behalf. He encouraged her by letting her know she was not alone. Yes, because of her specific position within the king's palace, Esther was uniquely qualified to carry out the mission alone. But, God didn't leave her alone. He offered sweet encouragement to her even during her feelings of inadequacy.

Our friend, Heather, recently found herself in a similar position of being uniquely qualified, yet seemingly alone, with overwhelming fears of inadequacy. She and her father Kyle, both doctors, were a part of a medical mission trip to Zimbabwe with the organization P.A.P.A. (Physicians Aiding Physicians Abroad), which Kyle founded and named for the endearing name his children call him. Only two days into their trip, Kyle cut himself while performing a surgical procedure on a confirmed AIDS patient.

Kyle's best hope was receiving anti-retrovirals, but finding the drugs in a remote area of Zimbabwe, acquiring them and administering them within a three-hour window of time proved challenging. The decision to take the drugs was fraught with emotion, as the drugs' side effects are numerous and sometimes even fatal. In the first of many miracles in this situation, they located the medicines, and Kyle was able to take them. Although he had immediate and serious side effects, Kyle continued to work the rest of the week performing many more C-sections and providing care to hundreds of sick patients. Finally, amidst labored breathing, dizziness, fever, and possible liver failure, an urgent return trip to America was crucial.

Following many stressful decisions, including leaving other family members behind, the first plane trip, and a 12-hour layover, Kyle's condition continued to worsen, and it appeared that his liver was beginning to fail. As Heather and Kyle boarded the final plane for the 17-hour flight to the States, it was apparent, even to the flight attendant, that Kyle was gravely ill. Heather explained to the attendant and eventually to the pilots, that she was a doctor and would take full responsibility for her papa. She expressed to them that it was highly possible her papa might die en route and that his only hope was to get to America as soon as possible.

The weight of responsibility began to settle on Heather. She felt completely inadequate at being the only doctor to make life or death decisions for her father over the next critical hours. She visited with Kyle about last messages he wanted to send to his other children and to his wife. As he drifted off to sleep, Heather retreated to the plane's tiny bathroom where she curled into a fetal position on the floor and wept, begging God for her papa's life.

When someone finally knocked on the door, she exited the restroom to find four men waiting in the galley area. One of them asked, in Spanish, if she needed some medicine. Heather politely declined and told them, in broken Spanish, that she didn't need medicine and that she was a doctor. At this information, the man's face brightened. They, too, were doctors and so were 96 other passengers on the flight! Heather asked them to pray, which they did. They also brought one of their colleagues to meet her and talk over Kyle's symptoms. This man just happened to be one of the top infectious disease doctors in Mexico. He offered to watch over Kyle while Heather got some sleep. When she awoke, Kyle was standing in the aisle talking to one of the Mexican doctors. While still very sick, Kyle's condition had improved dramatically. He continued to recover as they landed back in the States, and there was not a trace of HIV detected in his blood.

Heather related later,

> "The strangest thing is this: 'When confronted by death itself, my thought was not, '*Why did we come to Africa?*' but, '*Why didn't we come more often?*' I witnessed a miracle. I witnessed, firsthand, the power of prayer. If you have ever felt like me, that your contribution is too small, your prayers too inarticulate, and your sacrifice not weighty enough to matter, I hope this story inspires you. Your prayers do not fall on deaf ears, and they are not to a God who is distant and uninvolved. I cannot explain why God doesn't always answer in the ways we expect, but I can tell you that He is alive and well, He loves us deeply, and He saved Papa."

When we find ourselves in a hopeless, lonely situation with overwhelming responsibility weighing on us, we mustn't forget that the kind and compassionate God who Esther trusted is still working fascinating miracles in our lives today! He has used one woman's voice to encourage hundreds of believers in Persia with the melody of His amazing grace. He used 100 physicians who speak a foreign language to encourage one young woman praying for her papa. These women requested prayer and walked in obedience according to the unique position and talents given to them.

Consider your unique talents and the position God has placed you in as a neighbor, a co-worker, or a friend. God can miraculously use one voice to amplify His praise and to exponentially encourage His people just as

He used Esther in Persia, Susan's friend in the modern-day country of Persia we call Iran, and Heather in an airplane thousands of feet above the Atlantic Ocean.

16. What is God specifically calling you to do to bring Him glory and to encourage His people?

____

Have courage. God can use us. For perhaps we have come to a royal position as children of the King of Kings for "such a time as this" (Esther 4:13-14). Let us celebrate the mighty works of our King!

SUCH A CELEBRATION!

The Feast of Purim is a retelling of the story of Esther and is a time of great rejoicing. Purim falls on the 15th of Adar (late February or March), exactly one month before Passover. People dress in costumes and read the story of Esther in the synagogues. Every time the name of Haman is heard, it is vigorously booed. Noisemakers (groggers) are used to blot out his name. At each mention of Mordecai, everyone cheers!

One of the traditional foods is hamantashen (Haman's pockets or Haman's ears). These are triangular-shaped cookies with jelly or other sweet filling. It is also traditional to observe the fast of Esther from dawn to dusk the day before Purim, in order to remember that Esther and the Jewish population fasted before Esther presented herself, uninvited, before the king.

Interestingly, Purim is the one Jewish holiday when it is acceptable for the adults to have a little too much alcohol. In fact, one rabbinic tradition says that one should partake of the joy and drink until he doesn't know the difference between Mordecai and Haman! This may be a little extreme, but it does illustrate the great joy of deliverance felt by the Jews.

There are two very important mitzvot (plural of mitzvah, and pronounced mits-VOHT) associated with this holiday. A mitzvah

(MITS-vuh) literally refers to any of the 613 rabbinical commandments from the Torah that Jews are obligated to observe. There are other commandments, originating from rabbinical tradition, that take the number of mitzvot up to approximately 630. A mitzvah can also refer to any good deed. The two mitzvot associated with Purim are:

1. Matanot La'evyonim
This mitzvah requires every Jew to give gifts (charity) to at least two needy persons or worthy causes, teaching the lesson of showing gratitude by helping others who are less fortunate. Charity to the poor is a mitzvah from the Torah.

2. Mishloach Manot
This mitzvah involves sending at least two items of food to at least one person. This comes directly from Esther 9:19, "Therefore the Jews of the rural areas, who live in the rural towns, make the fourteenth day of the month Adar a holiday for rejoicing and feasting and sending portions of food to one another." This mitzvah is an example of one of the "other" commandments mentioned above.

The story of Esther is such a testimony to God's faithfulness to his chosen people. It is just one of the many examples of God keeping his promise to the offspring of Abraham.

Genesis 12:3 says,

> "I will bless those who bless you,
> And I will curse him who curses you;
> And in you all the families of the earth shall be blessed."

Through many faithful prayers, with one woman's courageous voice in a faraway land, God blessed His people. Let's celebrate that God did not forsake his chosen people; for the Messiah came through the lineage of the Jews. He protected them just as He promised, and He sent us a Savior who is faithful and true. Remembering God's safekeeping of us in the past makes it easier to confidently trust the promises He's made for our future. However, sometimes we find ourselves in such a chaotic mess, it's hard to remember God's faithfulness. Later generations of Jewish people found themselves in this very predicament during the time period between the writings of the Old Testament and the New Testament, as we shall see in the story of Hanukkah.

Hanukkah

SUCH A MESS!

Hanukkah is one of the Jewish feasts that most Christians have at least heard of probably because it occurs around the Christmas season. Many people mistakenly think of it as the "Jewish Christmas." This is not the case. This feast commemorates the cleansing and rededication of the second temple after Antiochus Epiphanes desecrated it.

Let's take a minute to get everyone on the same page historically. The Jews have returned from their Babylonian and Assyrian captivity. The temple has been rebuilt, and the Jews are again able to make sacrifices and keep the Jewish feasts. (This history is recorded in the books of Ezra and Nehemiah.) Then, in 322 B.C., Alexander the Great conquers the entire ancient world, including Israel, turning it into one Greek, or Hellenistic, empire.

Alexander the Great died without an heir, and his four generals divided his kingdom. The two generals who concern Israel are Ptolemy, who took the land south of Israel, including Egypt, and Seleucus, who took control of the land north of Israel, including Syria. There was a long series of battles between the kingdoms of Syria and Egypt over who would control Judea (Israel). In 171 B.C., Antiochus IV came to the Seleucid throne and ruled over Syria and Judea.

Antiochus considered himself to be a god, and therefore insisted on being called Antiochus Epiphanes which means "the visible God." The

Jews made a play on words and called him Epimanes, meaning "madman."

The Greek rulers sought to unify their kingdom by Hellenization, or assimilating everyone into the Greek culture. This required people to adopt the culture of the Greeks, including their religion which worshiped multiple Greek gods. (Remember Greek mythology from high school English? And you thought you'd never have a need for that information!) Most people were eager to accept the Greek culture. The Greeks were considered "enlightened" and, for the most part, people wanted to be like them. Traditional Jews however, did not want to give up their religion or culture.

In 168 B.C., Judaism was declared an illegal religion. The Jews could choose to give up their Jewish religion and customs or to die. Antiochus marched into Jerusalem, desecrated the temple, ordered that a pig be sacrificed on the altar, and erected a statue of Zeus as the focal point of worship in the temple. It is thought that the face of Zeus (Jupiter) was the likeness of Antiochus.

His method of forced assimilation was simple. A detachment of soldiers would march into a community and set up a pagan altar. They bribed the leaders of the community to sacrifice a pig on the pagan altar and eat pork. They assembled the townspeople and expected them to do the same. If the respected elders went first, then it was more likely that the others would follow. The soldiers tortured or killed anyone who did not partake in the sacrifice. They also killed anyone caught celebrating Sabbath, reading the Torah, or partaking in any Jewish activity, along with his or her family.

In one village where the soldiers began this routine of forced sacrifice, lived an old, godly priest named Mattathias (MataTHIGHus). The soldiers tried to bribe him to be the first to take part in the pagan ritual, but he refused. When another Jew came forward to sacrifice, Mattathias killed him, and a revolt started. This became known as the Maccabean revolt. It was named after Judah, the son of Mattathias, who took over upon the death of the elderly priest. Judah was known as "the Maccabee" meaning "the hammer."

Against great odds, the Maccabees recaptured Jerusalem in 165 B.C. on the 25th of Kislev (Kislev falls in December), exactly three years to the day after Antiochus desecrated the temple. The Maccabees immediately set out to restore the temple to the true worship of God. They restored the broken menorah, but they only found enough pure oil to burn for one day. It would take eight days to purify more oil. They decided to light the Menorah anyway, allowing the light of God to shine forth immediately. Amazingly, the oil burned for eight days until they were able to prepare more oil. So, Hanukkah celebrates the two miracles: the impossible military victory and the miraculous supply of oil.

Today, the traditional Jewish observance is an eight-day festival that has a nine-branch menorah, a Hanukkiyah (Hawn-a-KEY-a), as its focal point. The traditional menorah has seven branches, but the one used specifically for Hanukkah has nine branches. Eight of the candles represent the eight days of miraculous oil provided in the temple. The ninth branch, or candle, is called the shamash (SHAH-mish), or servant candle, and is used to light the other candles.

A great object lesson for kids is to have them each take a turn to be the Shamash or servant for the day and unselfishly help other members of the family. Each night, candles are placed in the hanukkiyah (starting at the right side) corresponding to the number of the day of Hanukkah. The servant candle is then lit and used to light the other candles (starting at the left). Before the lighting of the candles, a traditional prayer is recited. The family enjoys a festive meal together and sings traditional songs. Because of the miracle of oil, it is also traditional to eat foods cooked in oil such as latkes (potato pancakes) and Sufganiot (Israeli doughnuts).

Children play a game called dreydels. They take turns spinning a wooden top that has Hebrew letters on each of its four sides. The letters are nun, gimel, hey, and shin. They stand for the phrase "a great miracle happened there." They win or lose chocolate coins called gelt. This game originated at the time of the Greek rule over the Jews. When Judaism was declared illegal, the Jews still gathered together to study the Torah. If soldiers came upon the group, the men would hide the scrolls and appear to be gambling over a spinning dreydel. With any luck, they might get a soldier to join in and win a few coins off of him.

Dreydels and Gelt

It is interesting that the Jews, who celebrate Hanukkah, have no direct reference to it in the Tanakh (Old Testament). But the Christians, who do not celebrate it, have a clear reference to it in the New Testament.

Read John 10:22-33.

1. What feast were they celebrating (v. 22)?

____

2. What did the Jewish leaders ask Jesus (v. 24)?

____

____

3. Do you think the Jewish leaders were genuinely seeking to know if Jesus was the Messiah? Why or why not?

____

4. What characterizes someone who is one of "his sheep" (vv. 27-29)?

____

____

5. Are you one of His sheep?

____

We can assume from this passage that Jesus observed the feast of Hanukkah. And, He observed it in the same temple that was cleansed and rededicated by the Maccabees less than 200 years earlier. Jesus used this occasion to identify Himself as the Messiah. The Jewish leaders understood very clearly that Jesus was claiming to be equal with God, just as Antiochus Epiphanes had claimed during the Greek rule. In fact, the leaders were willing to stone Jesus for this outrageous claim.

SUCH A MIRACLE!

The Old Testament does not mention the feast of Hanukkah directly, but there are some amazing prophecies in Daniel fulfilled during this time period. Daniel gives a very accurate account of what happened in the battles between the King of the North and the King of the South even though it was written five centuries prior to the events.

Read Daniel 8:1-14.

1. What was the first animal Daniel saw (v. 3)?

____

2. What was the second animal Daniel saw (v. 5)?

____

3. What did the goat do to the ram (v.7)?

____

____

4. What happened to the large horn of the goat (v. 8)?

____

____

5. In verse 9, a small horn comes forth from one of the four horns. What does it do in verse 11?

____

____

____

6. In verse 12, why were the hosts given over to the horn?

____

This verse tells us that the trampling of the temple was caused by the sins of the people. The following verses give us some insight as to what those sins were:

Isaiah 42:24

> *"Who gave Jacob up for spoil and Israel to plunderers?*
> *Was it not the LORD, against whom we have sinned,*
> *And in whose ways they were not willing to walk,*
> *And whose law they did not obey?*
> *So He poured out on him the heat of His anger*
> *And the fierceness of battle; And it set him aflame all around ..."*

Malachi 1:7-10

> *"You place defiled food on my altar.*
> *But you ask, 'How have we defiled you?'*
> *By saying that the LORD's table is contemptible.*

> *When you bring blind animals for sacrifice, is that not wrong? When you sacrifice crippled or diseased animals, is that not wrong? Try offering them to your governor! Would he be pleased with you? Would he accept you?" says the LORD Almighty.*
>
> *"Now implore God to be gracious to us. With such offerings from your hands, will he accept you?" — says the LORD Almighty.*
>
> *"Oh, that one of you would shut the temple doors, so that you would not light useless fires on my altar! I am not pleased with you," says the LORD Almighty, "and I will accept no offering from your hands."*

Malachi 2:1

> *"And now this admonition is for you, O priests. If you do not listen, and if you do not set your heart to honor my name," says the LORD Almighty, "I will send a curse upon you, and I will curse your blessings. Yes, I have already cursed them, because you have not set your heart to honor me.*

So the Bible indicates that God allowed Antiochus to "trample on the temple" as a judgment for the sins of the people. To ensure that Daniel understood the vision, God interpreted it for him.

Read Daniel 8:20-25.

7. Who does the ram represent?

____

____

8. Who does the shaggy goat with one horn represent?

____

____

9. What is the meaning of the one horn being broken and four horns arising in its place?

____

____

Does this story sound familiar? Looking back historically, we realize that the events surrounding Alexander the Great fulfill the events of Daniel's vision. Even the actions of Antiochus are reported in great detail. He is the small horn mentioned in question number 9 above. He is also a type of the Antichrist who is yet to come. Daniel goes on to give more detail about the actions of Antiochus. As you read this, remember that Daniel prophesied these events about 500 years prior to their fulfillment.

Read Daniel 11:29-32.

10. Describe how this passage is similar to the events of Hanukkah you've learned about in this section.

____

____

____

____

The high priest, Yohanan, in Jerusalem, favored being ruled by Egypt over Syria due to less forceful Hellenization. His brother, Joshua (who changed his name to the Greek Jason), bribed Antiochus for the position of high priest. Jason had his brother assassinated. Three years later, Menelaus gained the high priest position by an even bigger bribe, and he was not even from the high priest family. He stole the golden vessels from the temple to pay the bribe.

Antiochus wanted to re-unify the empire as in the days of Alexander the Great. In 168 B.C., he went to war against Egypt, and victory seemed certain. The Roman senate intervened by dispatching Popillius Laenas to prevent Antiochus from capturing Egypt. "When asked if he wished peace or war with Rome, Antiochus stalled for time. The

Roman representative drew a circle in the sand around Antiochus and stated that he must decide before leaving the circle. Consequently, Antiochus was forced to withdraw from Egypt in great humiliation" (Howard & Rosenthal, 1997, p. 162).

This is just a sampling of the amazing detail God gave to Daniel about these and other events. Prophecy is a major component of the Old Testament. If the prophecy comes true, then it proves God's word is true. Repeatedly throughout history, God's word is proven to be true. We can trust that remaining prophecies will be fulfilled just as the previous ones have been.

The feast of Hanukkah celebrates the cleansing and re-dedication of the temple. The temple no longer stands as a house for the Spirit of God, but God's spirit dwells in each one of us who belong to Him.

A lot of people mistakenly try to make a direct connection between Hanukkah and Christmas. This is primarily because the two holidays occur at similar times. But these holidays celebrate two entirely different events: one, the birth of the promised Messiah, and the other, the deliverance of Israel from its oppressors. There is a more subtle connection between the two, however. If the revolt had not been successful, Antiochus would have wiped out the Jewish nation and no Jews would have been left from which a messiah could be born. This feast of Hanukkah celebrates the return of true temple worship of God, as His Spirit dwells in us. As Christians, we can observe the symbolism of this feast as a time to rededicate our lives to the worship of God and to ensure that our hearts are pure. For the Jews, this feast serves as a memorial to their past, but for us, it is a present reality and a hope for eternity. Just as the temple was purified after the time of Antiochus Epiphanes, our "temples" are made pure by the blood of Christ, the Messiah we celebrate at Christmas. That is the connection we have realized that authentically tie these two religious holidays together for us.

1 Corinthians 3:16 says, "Do you not know that you are a temple of God, and that the Spirit of God dwells in you?"

11. What parts of your life need to be cleansed or rededicated to the true worship of God?

____

____

____

As you continue to bring praise and worship to the Lord in your life's journeys, we pray that you will be feasting on the fascinating details of God's word and growing in your faith. Colossians 2:16-17 says, "Therefore let no one act as your judge in regard to food or drink or in respect to a festival or a new moon or a Sabbath day — things which are a mere shadow of what is to come; but the substance belongs to Christ."

Over the course of this study of the feasts of the Jewish faith, we have seen the substance of Christ in each of these feasts. We saw Jesus fulfill the weekly Sabbath by literally being our rest as we studied in Hebrews 3 and 4. We observed His literal fulfillment of the first three feasts collectively. He stayed true to the day, being crucified on Passover as the Jews were sacrificing their Passover lambs; He took on our sin, was wrapped in linen, and buried on the Feast of Unleavened Bread just as the Jews were hiding away their leaven representing sin; and finally, He rose again on the Feast of First Fruits as the first fruits of those who are asleep (1 Corinthians 15).

The beauty of these feasts is that they allow us to see so many aspects of God's character, and they illustrate so clearly the triune Godhead. We hope you have seen this wonderful portrayal throughout these feasts that God, the Father, composed in Leviticus 23. We observed Jesus, the Son, playing the lead role in fulfilling the first three feasts, and then we encountered the Holy Spirit as He took center stage at the Feast of Weeks by indwelling the apostles with His power. While the finale of the last three feasts seems yet to be unveiled, we considered some prefillments and several scenarios for the Messiah to step back on the world's stage by ultimately fulfilling the last three feasts of Trumpets, Day of Atonement, and Tabernacles when He again will set His foot upon the earth and tabernacle among men.

We hope your faith has been strengthened as we observed how God worked among His people through Old Testament heroes like Esther, the Maccabees in the time period between the Old and New Testaments, and through the stories and miracles of modern- day believers as well. Now that we have completed this journey with you, we, as always, along with all believers through the ages, eagerly await His imminent return as the King of Kings and the Lord of Lords. We look forward to the day that we, along with you, will be among those who say, "Blessed is He who comes in the name of the Lord."

Both of us, Carl and Dallas, pray that your life going forward will be an abundantly satisfying *Feast of Faith*!

> "I, Yeshua, have sent my angel to give you this testimony for the Messianic communities. I am the Root and Offspring of David, the bright Morning Star. The Spirit and the Bride say, 'Come!' Let anyone who hears say, 'Come!' And let anyone who is thirsty come, let anyone who wishes, take the water of life free of charge … The one who is testifying to these things says, 'Yes, I am coming soon!' Amen! Come, Lord Yeshua! May the grace of the Lord Yeshua be with all!" Revelation 22:16-17, 20-21. *Complete Jewish Bible* (Stern, 1998.)

Feast of Unleavened Bread				**Feast of Weeks**
Passover (Pesach)	**Unleavened Bread (Matzah)**	**First Fruits**		**Weeks (Shavuot)**
1st Month 14th Day	1st Month 15th Day	The day after Sabbath, during the Week of Unleavened Bread. This also begins the Counting of the Omer.	50 days	Also known as Pentecost; The day after the 7th Sabbath following First Fruits

Fulfillment by Jesus				**Fulfillment by the Holy Spirit**
Passover	**Unleavened Bread**	**First Fruits**		**Weeks**
Jesus' crucifixion 1 Corinthians 5:7	Jesus' burial 1 Corinthians 5:8	Jesus raised from the dead 1 Corinthians 15:20	50 days Ascension of Jesus	Gift of the Holy Spirit given Acts 2:1-13

Feast of Tabernacles (booths)

	Trumpets (Rosh Hashanah)	10 Days of Awe	Day of Atonement (Yom Kippur)		Tabernacles or Booths (Sukkot)	
3-4 month period	7th Month 1st Day		7th Month 10th Day	4 days	7th Month 15th Day Lasts 7 days	Shemini Atzeret (The assembly of the 8th day)

**These are just three varying possibilities for the fulfillment of these last three feasts. The bottom line is that we should live our lives as if Jesus is coming back today, and not be surprised if it's not exactly how we might be expecting it!*

Possible Fulfillments Yet to Come

	Trumpets	10 Days of Awe	Day of Atonement	Tabernacles	
3-4 month period	Rapture of Believers I Thes. 4:17		Tribulation Zech. 12:10-13:9	Second Coming, Millennium Zech. 14:4-9; Rev. 21:1-3	Shemini Atzeret
	Regathering of Jews to Israel Jer. 32:37-41; Ez. 36:24, 37:1-14		Second Coming; Israel will look upon the One they've pierced Zech. 3:9-10; 12:10; 13:1; 14:9; Zeph. 3:14-20	All will go to Jerusalem to celebrate the Feast of Tabernacles Zech. 14:16-19	
Current Church Age (Matt. 28:19-20, John 4:35)	Second Coming Zech. 14:4-9; Rev. 21:1-3	Tribulation (Zech. 12:10-13:9)	Great White Throne Judgment Rev. 20:11-15	New Heaven & New Earth Rev. 21:1-7; Zech. 14:10-11	Millennium Reign (Rev. 21:1-3)

SELECTED WORKS CITED

Austin, M. C. (Composer). (March 1912). In The Garden.

Bloomfield, A. E. (1976). *Where is the Ark of the Covenant?* Minneapolis, MN: Dimension Books.

Chapman, J. W., & Marsh, C. H. (Composers). (1910). One Day. [J. Johnson, Performer]

Cohen, A. (1949). *Everyman's Talmud.* New York, NY: Schocken Books, Inc.

DellaPergola, S. (2010). *World Jewish Population, 2010.* Jerusalem, Israel: Berman Institute-North American Jewish Data Bank University of Connecticut.

Eglesh, R. (2010, September 7). Nation's Population Closes in on 7.65 Million as 5770 Comes to an End. *Jerusalem Post*, p. 1.

Flavius Josephus, T. W. (1999). *The New Complete Works of Josephus.* Grand Rapids, MI: Kregel Publications.

Goldman, A. L. (2000). *Being Jewish.* New York, NY: Simon & Schuster, pp. 108, 115, 175.

Greenberg, B. (1983). *How to Run a Traditional Jewish Household.* New York, NY: Simon & Schuster, pp. 325, 341, 367, 466.

Herzog, C. (1984). *The Arab-Israeli Wars.* New York, NY: Random House, Inc, pp. 70, 230.

Howard, K., & Rosenthal, M. (1997). *The Feasts of the Lord.* Nashville: Thomas Nelson, Inc., pp. 107, 162.

Josephus, T. b. (1999). *The New Complete Works of Josephus.* (W. Whiston, Trans.) Grand Rapids, MI: Kregel.

KJV, Holy Bible. (1976). Nasville, TN: Thomas Nelson.

Kasdan, B. (1993). *God's Appointed Times.* Baltimore, MD: Messianic Jewish Publishers.

Larson, B. (2009, November 2). *Real Life.* Retrieved from beverly-larson.wordpress.com.

Lockman Foundation. (1998). *New American Standard Exhaustive Concordance of the Bible.* (R. L. Thomas, Ed.) Anaheim, CA: Foundation Publications, Inc., p. 1359.

Mishory, A. (2010). *www.jewishvirtuallibrary.org/jsource/History/isflag.html.* (A.-I. C. Enterprise, Producer) Retrieved 2011, from www.jewishvirtuallibrary.org.

Negev, A., & Gibson, S. (2001). *Archaeological Encyclopedia of the Holy Land.* New York, NY: Continuum Publishing Group.

Nelson's Royal Classics, Bunyan, John. (1999). *Pilgrim's Progress.* Nashville, TN: Thomas Nelson, Inc., p. 62.

NIV, International Bible Society. (1984). *The Holy Bible,* New International Version. Grand Rapids, MI: Zondervan.

Pearlman, M. (1988). *The Dead Sea Scrolls in the Shrine of the Book.* Jerusalem, Israel: Israel Museum Products, Ltd, p. 72.

Reagan, D. R. (1998, May). The Gate to Prophecy. *The Lamplighter* , p. 6.

Reagan, D. R. (2011). *Lamb & Lion Ministries*. Retrieved from lamblion.com.

Ritmeyer, L. &. (2002). *The Ritual of the Temple in the Time of Christ*. Jerusalem, Israel: Carta, The Israel Map and Publishing Company, Ltd.

Sachar, H. M. (1998). *A History of Israel from the Rise of Zionism to Our Time*. New York, NY: Alfred A. Knopf, pp. 320-321.

Schmalz, R. E. (1999). *The Messianic Seal of the Jerusalem Church*. Tiberias, Israel: Olim Publications.

Stern, D. H. (1990). *Restoring the Jewishness of the Gospel*. Clarksville, MD: Jewish New Testament Publications, Inc, p. 7.

Stern, D. (1998). *The Complete Jewish Bible*. Clarksville, MD: Jewish New Testament Publications, Inc.

The Message Bible. (2004). Colorado Springs, CO: Navpress.

The New American Standard Bible. (1977). LaHabra California: The Lockman Foundation.

Therese of Lisieux, S. (1996). *Story of a Soul: The Autobiography of St. Therese of Lisieux*. (F. J. Clarke, Trans.) Washington D.C.: ICS Publication.

Whitman, W. (1865). *O Captain! My Captain!* New York: New York Saturday Press.

Zodhiates, S. T. (1992). *The Complete Word Study Dictionary: New Testament*. Chattanooga, TN: AMG Publishers, pp. 59, 884.

Zola Levitt Ministries. (2011). Retrieved from Levitt.com

NOTES

NOTES

NOTES

NOTES

NOTES

NOTES

NOTES

www.FeastsofFaith.com